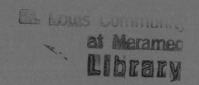

ALHAMBRA

ALHAMBRA

TEXT BY MICHAEL JACOBS
PHOTOGRAPHS BY FRANCISCO FERNÁNDEZ

RIZZOLI
NEW YORK

To Juan Antonio Díaz,
and in memory of David Jacobs and María Sanchez

First published in the United States of America in 2000 by
Rizzoli International Publications, Inc.
300 Park Avenue South, New York, NY 10010

ISBN: 0-8478-2251-6

LC: 99-80009

Set in Syndor by Frances Lincoln Limited

Printed in and bound in Hong Kong

PAGE 1 The Court of the Lions
PAGES 2-3 A view of the Alhambra from the Albaicín
RIGHT A painting by Richard Ford showing a pillar in
an anteroom of the Hall of the Ambassadors
OPPOSITE A detail of decorative tiles

C
O
N
T
E
N
T
S

INTRODUCTION

The palace city of the Alhambra, frequently described as a great ship moored between the mountains and the plains, is also a monument poised uneasily between myth and reality.

Travellers, overwhelmed by its honeycomb forms, its profusion of fantastical ornament, the sensuality of its gardens and fountains and the beauty of a setting in which lush vegetation is profiled against peaks of Alpine grandeur, have been lulled into a dream-like state in which the Alhambra has emerged as the poetical embodiment of a glorious Islamic civilization at its artistic zenith. Viewed more dispassionately, however, the Alhambra could also be seen as the spectacular public relations exercise of a desperate, insecure and relatively minor dynasty constantly threatened by extinction.

What is more, in its present state, the monument that has inspired so many fairy-tale delusions gives only a partial and misleading idea of a site that once comprised not only palaces but also a densely crowded group of government and military buildings, modest houses and artisan workshops. Of this former Islamic city, there remain only the fortress and fortifications, and a fragmentary palace complex which, though forming the most important survival in the world of a medieval Islamic palace, has been ravaged to such an extent by disasters, alterations, neglect and drastic restoration that comparatively little has been left of the original structure and polychrome colouring and virtually nothing of the furnishings (for a map of the present layout of the Alhambra see pages 184–5).

That the most beautiful parts of the Alhambra have survived at all is in fact a miracle, for, in a paradox first spelt out by the French traveller Théophile Gautier in 1845, almost all of the magnificent ornamentation was crafted 'neither in marble nor alabaster, nor even in humble stone', but rather in the cheaper and more easily destructible materials of plaster, wood and tiles. Though intended to dazzle, the palace complex of Granada's Islamic rulers was probably created with no more of an eye to the future than were the Mongolian conqueror Tamerlane's tent palaces in bejewelled gold cloth. An awareness of the fragility that underlies all this splendour, far from shattering illusions, as Gautier imagined, has merely supplied an added poignancy to a monument whose very insubstantiality seems to have encouraged writers to cloak it in a heavy mantle of clichés and tedious superlatives.

A detail of a window in the Court of the Myrtles.

Few places in Europe arouse so many heightened expectations as the Alhambra; and, inevitably, the first-time response of many of today's visitors, particularly those arriving on rushed day trips from the Spanish coast, is one of disappointment. The famous halls and water-filled patios appear smaller than they do in the imagination; the crowds can often be unbearable; and the whole has such an air of familiarity as to seem at times barely distinguishable from the thousands of imitations it has spawned. Even Richard Ford, whose celebrated *Handbook to Spain* of 1845 contains one of the most passionate early appraisals of the Alhambra, warned of the dangers of 'an over-exaggerated notion of a place which from the dreams of boyhood has been fancy-formed'. 'Few airy castles of illusion,' he concluded, 'will stand the prosaic test of reality' – an opinion that was echoed shortly afterwards by his travelling compatriot Charles Cayley, who wrote of the Alhambra in 1854 that 'nothing earthly can bear the fatal ordeal of a previous reputation'.

The mythology that has grown up around the Alhambra is difficult to ignore, and indeed must itself be explored if we are fully to comprehend why this monument – reputedly the most visited tourist site in the world after the Taj Mahal – has exerted an infinitely greater appeal than the better preserved and artistically far more innovative Great Mosque at Córdoba. However, it is only through trying to separate the real Alhambra from its mythical superstructure that we can begin to see the monument afresh, and to view it as a puzzle of engrossing complexity that demands an enormous amount of time and patience to appreciate. The influential Victorian travel writer Augustus Hare, who considered the Alhambra 'the most perfectly beautiful place in the world', was quite right in insisting that many visits were required to understand the place properly: it is a monument that was designed to be seen under different lights, and to leave the viewer with the impression that a wealth of tiny details and secret corners remains always to be discovered.

Conflicting academic theories and interpretations, misleading inscriptions, confusions caused by ill-informed restorations, a lack of literary documentation and a tantalizingly fragmented and still far from complete body of archaeological evidence have all to be dealt with when trying to picture what the Alhambra was originally like. At times we might wonder if in stripping the monument of centuries of falsifications and delusions we are divesting the place of much of its glamour and exoticism. Yet such is the Alhambra's enduring fascination that the further we cast the cold light of scholarship, the greater the mysteries that are exposed.

THE SHINING RAYS OF THE FULL·MOON

The Alhambra and Islamic Spain

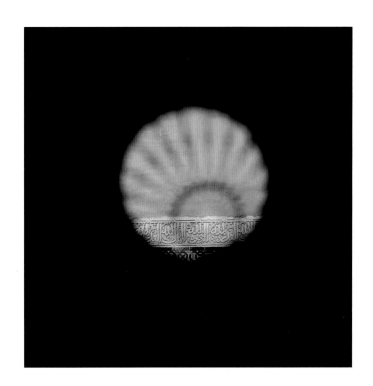

ABOVE A fleeting effect of light within the Alhambra's Mexuar.

LEFT A view of the Alhambra from the Albaicín, as seen under the ideal moonlit conditions dreamt of by romantic travellers.

THE STATESMAN AND SCHOLAR IBN AL-KHATIB, a key witness to the Alhambra in its heyday, gave his invaluable account of Islamic Granada and its rulers the poetic title of *The Shining Rays of the Full Moon*. This might not have been the most suitable title for what was essentially a scholarly work dealing with mediocre and intrigue-filled lives, but it was one that encapsulated the mythical glow that has coloured so many perceptions of Islamic Spain.

The Alhambra cannot be studied in isolation from the long history of myths, half-truths and romantic distortions that have grown up since the time of the Islamic conquest of Spain early in the 8th century. Appropriately this history has its origins in one of the most widely known legends of the Spanish Middle Ages – the story of the locked chamber which none of Spain's Visigothic kings was allowed to enter. The king whose curiosity led him eventually to do so was Roderick, who found walls painted with armed Arab horsemen and an urn standing on a silver and gold table that had belonged to King Solomon. Within the urn was a scroll of parchment warning that 'whenever this chamber is violated … the people painted on these walls will invade Spain, overthrow its kings, and subdue the entire land'.

This glamorous story shielded, of course, a rather unattractive reality. King Roderick brought about the collapse of his country not through any single daring or foolhardy act but through many years of incompetent and unpopular rule. Spain, weakened by economic problems, political and religious divisions, and the dissatisfaction of an increasingly persecuted Jewish community, became an obvious target for Islamic powers keen on maintaining the momentum of conquest after the death of the prophet Muhammad in 636.

In 711, ten years after North Africa had been taken by the Muslims, a small Berber force led by the Arab general Tariq Ibn Ziryab crossed from Tangier and seized Gibraltar. Despite the smallness of this invading army, most of Spain was brought under Islamic control by as early as 720, by which stage a high proportion of the country's indigenous inhabitants had adopted Islamic customs and religion.

The extraordinary speed with which all this took place reflects the extent of Roderick's unpopularity no less than the military genius of the Muslims. The king's numerous Jewish and Christian opponents were easily won over by the invaders, who allowed them to retain their property and offered considerable financial rewards to those wishing to convert to Islam.

In the Spain of today, where it has become fashionable to stress an affinity with the Muslim past, the ease of the Spanish assimilation of Islam is sometimes also attributed to a strong African element in the country's ethnic make-up long before 711. The relative scarcity of documents relating to the beginnings of Islamic rule in Spain, and the fact that most of the first accounts of the conquest were written at a much later period by Christian and Islamic fanatics, have undoubtedly led to simplified and exaggerated versions of Spanish history. One of the most popular misconceptions – encouraged by the tendency of Christian sources to use the blanket

A lone Moorish flag rises over Granada in this *portulano,* or coastal map, of Spain drawn up in 1375 by the Jewish cartographer Cresques of Majorca.

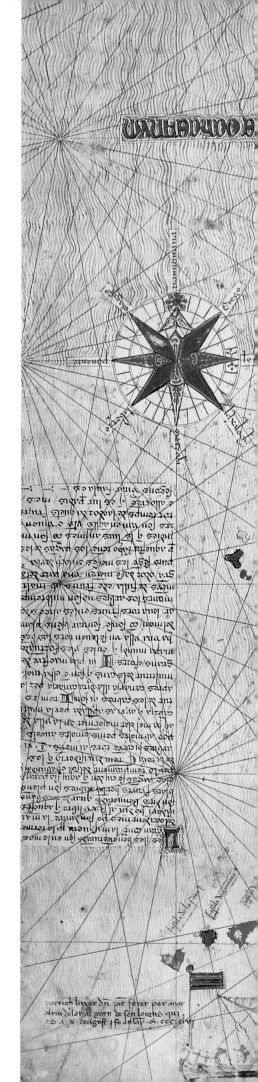

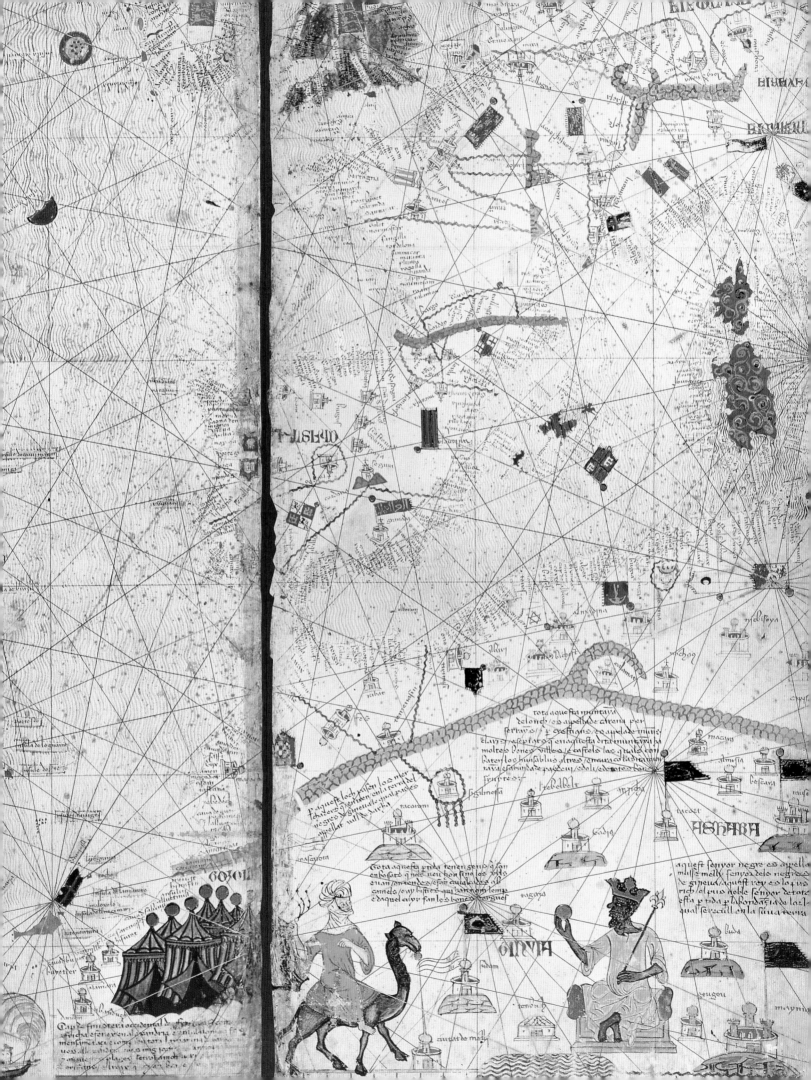

ABOVE Moorish warriors of different tribes are portrayed in this 11th-century manuscript of the Apocalypse.

OPPOSITE Originally a modest structure built around 780 by Abd al-Rahman I, the Great Mosque at Córdoba grew in tandem with the dramatic expansion of the town itself, the last additions being made at the end of the 10th century by the all-powerful Umayyad chamberlain al-Mansur. The atmospherically lit interior, with its multitude of columns disappearing into the darkness, has been compared to a forest since at least the time of the 19th-century French traveller Théophile Gautier.

term 'Moors' for the Islamic settlers – is to think of the settlers as representing a united and harmonious front. In fact they formed a very mixed and divided group made up of an élite Arab minority, a Berber majority and numerous Syrians, Egyptians and Yemenis. This ethnic diversity was further complicated by growing numbers of *muslimah* (Muslim converts), *muwalladun* (the offspring of marriages between Muslim men and Christian women) and *saqaliba* (slaves of European origin who had been indoctrinated into Arab ways). Unsurprisingly, 'al-Andalus', as Spain was now called by the Muslims, was soon beset by continual in-fighting that threatened the country's stability.

Al-Andalus might indeed have collapsed as suddenly as it had risen if it had not been for the arrival in Córdoba in 756 of Prince Abd al-Rahman, sole surviving member of the Umayyad family from Damascus. For over 150 years the Umayyads, as the legitimate successors of Muhammad and 'Commanders of the Faith', had ruled the whole Islamic world from Damascus under the title of caliph. In 750 Caliph Marwan II was deposed and killed and his family massacred at a banquet, from which, miraculously, Abd al-Rahman managed to escape. After wandering incognito through the Near East and North Africa, he eventually raised enough support to bring an army over to Spain, which attracted him as a place desperately in need of a strong ruler. Here he established the Umayyad dynasty in Córdoba, and took on the government of al-Andalus by appointing himself emir. In 929 his descendant Abd al-Rahman III, who had to dye his hair black in order to emphasize his Arab ancestry, assumed the title of caliph, and inspired the greatest period in the history of Islamic Spain.

The first detailed description of 10th-century Córdoba was written as late as 1632 by the Egyptian historian al-Maqqari, whose vision of the city was obviously affected by nostalgia for the lost glories of Islam. But though it is impossible to believe that Córdoba had once been a metropolis containing, in al-Maqqari's estimate, 1,600 mosques, 900 public baths, 60,300 mansions for the wealthy, 213,077 ordinary homes and 80,455 shops, it was indisputably a city of extraordinary size and splendour, rivalled only by Damascus, to which it was often compared.

A surviving testimony to Córdoba's cultural brilliance is its Great Mosque or Mezquita. This became the model for some of the major mosques of North Africa, and clearly shows the degree to which the art and architecture of al-Andalus had ceased by the 10th century to be a slavish emulation of eastern prototypes. A masterly example of the application of western elements to an eastern framework, with super-imposed rows of arches imitative of Roman aqueducts, the building also greatly encouraged the Muslim trend towards an architecture in which the distinction between structure and decoration becomes ever more blurred. This is particularly evident in the sensational additions made to the mosque during the time of Abd al-Rahman III's successor al-Hakkam II, when ornamentation of breathtaking intricacy was combined with forms of revolutionary complexity, such as star-shaped vaults and superimposed lacework arches.

Córdoba's Mezquita was ranked by early travellers as one of the great wonders of the world, as was the outlying palace city of Medina Azahara, which was begun in 939, and – according to al-Maqqari – involved in its construction no fewer than 10,000 workers and 1,500 beasts of burden. Conceived as a summer palace for Abd al-Rahman III, Medina Azahara was actually a vast architectural complex featuring several palaces, a mosque, gardens, a zoo, an aviary and weapons factories. As with the Mezquita, no expense was spared on materials: marble was imported from Almería and Carthage, and engraved basins from Constantinople and Syria; the roof tiles were covered in gold and silver. In this respect, no greater contrast can be imagined than with the Alhambra, which, though almost certainly inspired by the example of Medina Azahara, used the ephemeral medium of stucco to try to reproduce the effects of genuinely rich materials. The irony is that whereas the fragile shell of the Alhambra has managed to remain standing over the centuries, the solid stone-walled Medina Azahara was razed to the ground by an enraged mob in 1009, and survives to this day only as a jigsaw puzzle of excavated fragments.

The civil and political unrest that destroyed Medina Azahara also shattered Umayyad rule in Spain, and was responsible for rescuing from obscurity the town at the foot of the Alhambra hill – Granada. Up to the early 11th century this town was a minor settlement subordinate to the then district capital of Elvira (the Roman Illiberis), which lay 12½ miles (20 km) north-west, in the middle of the broad fertile valley known as the *vega*. With the ousting of the Umayyads from Spain in 1031, the place became the capital of one of the twelve petty kingdoms or *taifas* into which al-Andalus came to be divided.

The rulers of this kingdom were the Berber dynasty of the Zirids, who had been granted the governorship of the province of Elvira in 1014. According to their own, later, claims they had been invited here to guard the inhabitants from the rampaging Berber armies who had swept through the area after 1009. In fact they themselves were probably little different from these other Berbers, and are more likely to have seized power than to have been offered it.

Shortly after coming to Elvira, the founder of the Zirid dynasty, Zawi Ibn Ziri, transferred the entire population of this exposed, low-lying town to the better-protected settlement of Granada, which is situated on the lower slopes of Spain's highest mountain range, the Sierra Nevada. The defensive advantages of the new site were matched by what the great popularizer of the Alhambra, Washington Irving, would characterize as a 'combination of delights so rare in a southern city – the fresh vegetation and temperate airs of a northern climate, with the vivacious ardours of a tropical sun, and the cloudless azure of a southern sky'.

The earliest Islamic commentators were no less enthusiastic about Granada's situation, and frequently compared it in its sensual charms to those of Damascus. The geographer Ahmad Ibn Muhammad Ibn Muza al-Razi, writing in the 10th century, praised the Sierra Nevada for its abundance of springs, flowers and cool resting places. In the 1090s 'Abd Allah, last of the Zirid kings, evoked the excitement of his ancestors on contemplating for the first time from Granada a panoramic view over a 'beautiful plain full of streams and wooded groves'. As well as reflecting the

This eloquent fragment from the originally three-arched Zirid bridge known as the Puente del Cadi was built to cross the fast-flowing Darro, which separates the Alhambra from the Albaicín.

security concerns of a society in a constant state of alert, the move from Elvira to Granada signalled the beginnings of a mythology that would transform the Alhambra and its surroundings into an earthly paradise.

In contrast to Córdoba or even Damascus, where an Islamic urban framework had to be grafted on to a Roman infrastructure, Granada was a purpose-built Islamic city that developed around a core comprising a medina or commercial quarter and a fortress containing the ruler's palace. The Zirids established the latter in what became the district of the Albaicín, which faces the Alhambra hill across the narrow, fast-flowing stream of the River Darro. The few traces of early Islamic Granada are mainly to be found in this district, and include some of the masonry from the Zirid's palace, a 10th-century minaret (now the church tower of San José), and a superbly evocative bath complex incorporating Roman, Visigothic and Umayyad capitals. In addition there is the ruined arch of a bridge (much appreciated during the Romantic era) that forms part of a defensive wall joining the Albaicín fortress with an earlier castle on the western end of the Alhambra hill, a site occupied today by the Alhambra's Torre de la Vela.

This earlier castle, crowning the hill that was known to the Moors as the Sabika, probably dates back to at least Visigothic times, and indeed has been convincingly identified with a place referred to by Muslim commentators as 'Stephen's Castle', which housed an important Visigothic basilica dedicated to St Stephen. The name 'Alhambra', which derives from the Arabic 'al-Qalat al-Hamra' ('the red castle'), first appears in a late 9th-century document describing a skirmish earlier in the century between the local population and Arab troops loyal to the emir in Córdoba. The reddening of the castle's white stucco walls as a result of the high iron content in the local earth almost certainly accounts for this new name. However, a more romantic explanation involves a further incident between Arabs and locals in which the former, taking refuge once again inside the Alhambra, were forced to repair the walls at night by the red light of torches.

Largely abandoned during the first decades of Zirid rule in Granada, the 'red castle' was rebuilt and extended between 1052 and 1056 by the Jewish vizier or first minister Samuel Nagralla, who did so in order to safeguard the Jewish community who lived on one of the sides of the hill, and had given the original settlement of Granada the name of Gharnatat al-Yahud or 'Granada of the Jews'. Nagralla, whose family had been forced to flee their home in Córdoba in 1012, seems to have promoted in Granada a taste for Córdoban art, and it is significant that he placed in the reconstructed Alhambra a beautifully carved basin (now in the Alhambra Museum) possibly taken from Medina Azahara.

The desire to recreate the lost glories of Medina Azahara might well have been the ambition of Nagralla's son and successor, Yusuf, who came to power in 1056, and – if a theory put forward in the 1960s by the Jewish scholar F. Bargebuhr is to be believed – created alongside the castle a magnificent palace complex rivalling the one that would be built from the 13th century onwards by Granada's Nasrid rulers. Bargebuhr's fascinating theory, which is utterly unsupported by any archaeological evidence, has as its basis a description by the 11th-century Jewish poet Ibn Gabirol of a fountain of lions comparable to the fountain to be seen today in the Alhambra's famous Court of the Lions. Whether true or not, the idea of a lost palace complex on the site of the present buildings introduces the first alluring note of mystery into the Alhambra's tangled history.

The presence of a splendid Jewish palace on top of the Sabika hill might explain the growing resentment against the Jews that began now to be felt among the rest of Granada's population. In 1066 the local lawyer Abu Ishaq expressed his disgust at the way 'these Jews are meddling in [Granada's] affairs'; and, later that year, a pogrom was initiated in which Yusuf and many other of his co-religionists were killed. Zirid Granada itself had not long to live, for the town soon came to be threatened by the newly formed fanatical Berber sect of the Almoravids, who came to Spain in 1086 determined to bring under control a country they perceived as having succumbed to decadence and relaxed religious morals.

The Zirid king 'Abd Allah, in an extraordinary autobiography that brings vividly to life the last years of *taifa* Spain, wrote how his concerns about the 'possible consequences' of the Almoravid invasion made him realize the utmost urgency of 'doing something about my castles, not simply by restoring them and stocking them with provisions, but also by dealing with their weak and corrupt governors'. However, despite strengthening the Alhambra and all the other key fortifications of his small domain, 'Abd Allah eventually came to share the defeatist approach shown by his subjects, most of whom, he sensed, had come to feel that they were worse off under him than they would be under the Almoravids. Surrendering therefore without a fight in 1090, he was forced to leave behind in his Albaicín palace a great treasury of coins, gold, gems, glassware and rich fabrics, the discovery of which by the simple-living Berbers from the desert must have reinforced notions of the spoilt and sybaritic Spaniards. 'Abd Allah went into exile in Morocco, where, as he described in the closing pages of his memoirs, he reflected on human destiny, and found relief from melancholy in the simple pleasures of sex and bathing, but none at all in wine, which merely 'reminds the drinker of his sorrows'. Remarkably, he professed not to have given in to nostalgia, unlike his Sevillian contemporary the poet-king al-Mutamid, who suffered a similar fate, going into exile in the remote Moroccan town of Aghmat (where he was later to die) and bemoaning his fate with an intensity that brings to mind the outpourings of romantic historians as they evoke the loss of Islamic Spain. Instead 'Abd Allah was refreshingly down-to-earth: 'I personally believe,' he wrote, 'that there is no point in regretting the past . . . and that to make yourself ill for something that no longer exists is to tire yourself out and torment yourself just for the sake of it.'

ABOVE A later inscription records that this superlative marble basin, dating from the late 10th century, was taken from one of the Córdoban palaces belonging to the ruler al-Mansur. Brought over to the Alhambra during the Zirid period, this was placed in 1305 by Muhammad III at the entrance to the Alcazaba (the kernel of the present-day Alhambra), where it remained well into the 19th century. The motif of attacking lions was probably intended to symbolize the power of the caliphs.

OVERLEAF The Alcazaba is seen here in the late afternoon, when the redness of its walls becomes ever more pronounced.

With the departure of the Zirids, Granada entered a period of its history when little of architectural note was produced. The Almoravids, whose principal contribution to the Alhambra seems to have been the razing of the Visigothic church of St Stephen, were followed little more than sixty years later by the no less fanatical Berber sect of the Almohads. The latter, though responding to the sophisticated Andalucían environment with such a building as Seville's Giralda, advocated an essentially austere and sturdy architectural style utterly unlike the frail and exuberantly decorative one that would succeed it. Appropriately most of the major surviving Almohad structures in Spain are defensive ones, including the Torres Bermejas in Granada, which were built over 11th-century foundations on a south-western spur of the Sabika hill.

The burgeoning of fortresses in al-Andalus from the 11th century onwards was indicative of the growing insecurity of a country facing both internal conflicts and the steady advance of the conquering Christian armies from the north. After 1212,

following the catastrophic defeat of the Almohads at a battle known in Spanish as Las Navas de Tolosa, and in Arabic as *al-'Iqab* or 'the punishment', the Muslims finally ceased to be a major political power in Spain. Al-Andalus, reduced within a matter of years to a fraction of its former extent, became once again a fragmented country, as local leaders carved out for themselves their own rival domains.

The main hope for a unified al-Andalus, or indeed for the continuing survival of Muslim rule on Spanish soil, lay initially in a man claiming ancestry from the Hudid dynasty of *taifa* Zaragoza, Ibn Hud al-Judhami, who, rallying his supporters under the black banner of the dynasty that supplanted the Umayyads in Damascus, the Abbasids, soon gained control over much of Valencia and Murcia and present-day Andalucía. However, it was Ibn Hud's great enemy Muhammad Ibn Yusuf Ibn Nasr who, from far less promising beginnings, would eventually secure for two centuries the survival of al-Andalus.

The Torres Bermejas or Red Towers, which are separated from the Alhambra proper by what is now a wooded valley, once stood guard over the town's Jewish quarter. Dating possibly to as far back as the late 8th century, and as such Granada's earliest surviving defensive structures, they were entirely rebuilt by the Zirids and again by the Nasrid ruler Muhammad II. They are shown here against the background of Granada's southern suburbs.

Ibn Nasr features among the first ten
Nasrid rulers portrayed in the central
ceiling panel of the late 14th-century
Palace of the Lions.

'A great man, in every sense, was the founder of the Nasrid dynasty. His presence was fine and commanding, his manner bland and amiable, his courage worthy of the heroic age,' wrote the late 19th-century historian and eulogizer of the Alhambra, Albert F. Calvert. This glamorous image of Ibn Nasr, so typical of romantic attitudes in general towards Islamic Spain, is belied by Ibn al-Khatib's description of him as an illiterate man who wore sandals and coarse cloth, and came from a long line of farmers based in the insignificant small town of Arjona in Jaén province.

Furthermore, Ibn Nasr's impetuous and irascible character hardly lives up to the romantic view of the Nasrids as the benign upholders of religious tolerance in the face of growing Catholic fanaticism. As the proud descendant of one of the prophet Muhammad's immediate disciples, as well as the creator of a sovereign dynasty which claimed the same supreme authority and semi-religious character as the Umayyads, he espoused such a rigidly orthodox form of Islam that he once threatened to hack off the hands of a poet who, during ritual prayers, raised them to a height unacceptable to these particular beliefs.

Ibn Nasr's greatness lay principally in his political wiliness and opportunism, which made him one of the most unreliable allies of his day. His extraordinary rise to power began in his native Arjona during the Ramadan of 1232. With everyone gathered for Friday prayers, he persuaded the crowd to elect him as sultan. He then proceeded to win the allegiance of the nearby town of Jaén, whose inhabitants felt they could no longer rely on Ibn Hud to protect them from the fate recently suffered by neighbouring Ubeda, which had been captured in 1230 by Ferdinand III of Castile. Ibn Nasr soon came into direct conflict with Ibn Hud by gaining first Córdoba and then Seville; but he barely had time to enjoy either of these victories before the townspeople concluded that even the leadership of Ibn Hud was preferable to the humiliation of being ruled by someone from so provincial a place as Arjona. By 1234 Ibn Nasr had decided that the only way forward for him was to become a vassal to his long-term rival, though this did not stop him, two years later, from taking the side of Ferdinand III during the latter's successful siege of Córdoba.

In 1237, a few months after winning over the town of Granada, Ibn Nasr's way forward was cleared by the treacherous assassination of Ibn Hud by one of his protégés. Granada became the capital of Ibn Nasr's kingdom eight years later, after the Christians had conquered from him both Arjona and, more importantly, Jaén. Despite the loss of these towns, Ibn Nasr had by then extended his mountainous domain down to the Andalucían coast, to create a territory stretching all the way from the Straits of Gibraltar to north of Almería.

That he managed to hold on to this kingdom at a time when the remaining Muslim possessions in Spain had been captured by the Christians is due in part to the misguided policies of Ferdinand III's successor, Alfonso X, whose reputation as 'the Wise' was contradicted by the distinctly foolish concentration of his political efforts on a costly and futile pursuit of a military campaign in North Africa, and on his bid to become Holy Roman Emperor. Nor would Granada have been an easy conquest. The kingdom's terrain was wild and mountainous, and the wily Ibn Nasr remained as adept as ever in the dangerous game of changing allegiances.

Immediately after losing Jaén, Ibn Nasr made an act of feudal submission to Ferdinand III, which involved a large annual contribution to what was essentially a Christian protection racket, and also obliged him to take part personally in 1248 in the successful Christian siege of Seville. The protection of the Christians proved useful not least in guarding Ibn Nasr from a rebellious element within his own family, but it inevitably made numerous Muslim enemies for him, especially among those theologians who insisted that it was against Koranic law for an Islamic state to exist in submission to rulers of another faith.

Constantly balancing the demands of his different opponents, Ibn Nasr, in later life, ended up by antagonizing the Christians through enlisting the support of a new powerful tribe in Morocco, the Merinids, in whom many Muslims placed their hopes for a renewed Islamic onslaught on Spain. That Ibn Nasr was himself only too conscious of his shifty behaviour seems evident from his reputed reply to those sycophants who hailed him as a conqueror on his return to Granada after his morally questionable success at Seville in 1248. 'There is no conqueror but God,' he announced. These words became a family motto that would be inscribed all over the walls of a monument now beginning to take on a greater importance than ever before, the Alhambra.

An anonymous Islamic document records that in 1238, shortly after coming to Granada, Ibn Nasr climbed up to 'the site known as the "Alhambra"', and, after inspecting it, marked out the foundations of a new citadel. The walls were completed by the end of the year. At the same time he had an irrigation channel dug out that brought water from the Darro down through the future summer palace of the Generalife and on to the foot of the citadel. Previously the Alhambra had had to make do with rainwater collected in a cistern and with what water could be carried in pails along the defensive wall connecting the Alhambra with the Albaicín.

The creation of what came to be referred to in the 16th century as 'the Sultan's Canal' was obviously an essential step in the transformation of the Alhambra from an austere and purely defensive structure into a luxuriant palace city comparable not just to Medina Azahara but also to such Roman complexes as the Emperor Diocletian's celebrated palace at Split. Whether Ibn Nasr was himself responsible for commissioning such a complex on top of the Sabika hill is not known. While he is generally thought to have abandoned the Zirids' Albaicín palace in favour of rooms in the Alhambra's newly built keep, there is no evidence whatsoever to support the theory of a royal residence erected by him on the site of the future Palace of Charles V. What is certain, however, is that work on a palace city on the Alhambra hill was being carried out during the reign of his elder son and successor, Muhammad II, who came to power in 1273 after his father's death in a riding accident. Madinat al-Hamra, as this new city was called, stood in relation to Granada as later Versailles did to Paris, and indeed would enjoy the status of a separate township well into the Christian times, when it was ruled – up to as late as 1715 – by its own governor.

A ray of light striking one of the walls in the Palace of Comares illuminates the Nasrid motto, 'There is no conqueror but God.'

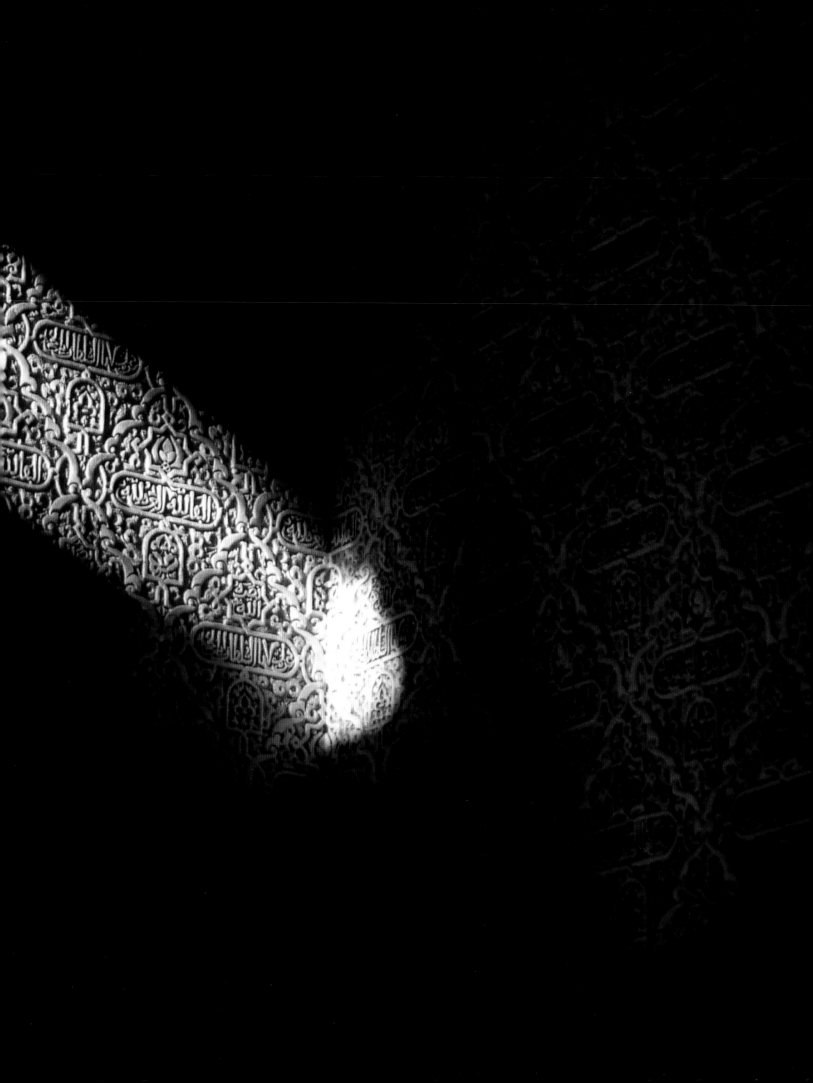

The exact chronological development of the palace city of the Alhambra is hard to determine, even with the help of surviving inscriptions, which can be used to date the decoration of a particular wall but not necessarily the underlying structure. Furthermore some of the inscriptions were moved around in the course of restoration in the 19th century, and at least one – in the Peinador de la Reina – appears to have been altered in the 14th century to obliterate the memory of the original patron. What becomes clear is that the palace city evolved through a process of continual remodelling and demolition, so much so that the original 13th-century complex – which included, in addition to the Citadel or Alcazaba, the royal cemetery or *rauda*, the Puerta del Vino, the so-called Palace of the Abencerrages and much of the medina – had already been extensively changed by the beginning of the following century.

Understandably, writers on the Alhambra have felt obliged to flesh out our slender knowledge of the Alhambra's complex history with tales of the violent and intrigue-filled lives of Ibn Nasr's successors. But in dwelling on the picturesque detail at the expense of the overall picture they have sometimes failed to show how the palace city of the Alhambra developed against the background of a society learning to assert its Islamic identity in the face of encroaching Christianity. Paradoxically, this monument, which would come to symbolize the essence of Islamic civilization, was started at a time when Islamic Granada was at its most blatantly westernized.

Ibn al-Khatib wrote how the 13th-century inhabitants of the sultanate wore clothes identical to those of their Christian neighbours, used exactly the same weaponry, flags and saddles, and generally shunned the use of turbans (not even the sultan himself had one). In later centuries, however, despite some persistence of Christian influence (Christmas, for instance, continued to be celebrated widely), customs and costumes became ever more oriental, as more and more Muslims moved here from other parts of Spain, and Granada took on an increasingly defiant stance to the Christians in the face of its growing isolation from the mainstream of Islam.

Significantly, the Alhambra as we know it today, was essentially the creation of the 14th century, when Nasrid Granada had finally begun to develop a greater degree of confidence and autonomy. An awareness of the great days of the Córdoban caliphate intensified, and certainly influenced the new image of strength and independence that Granada's rulers were now so anxious to sustain and promote. Inspired by the example of the Umayyads, artists and architects gradually abandoned the puritanical legacy of the Almohads, and started to revive and elaborate forms evolved in 10th-century Córdoba. The parallels between the Alhambra and Medina Azahara must have seemed now greater than ever.

The first surviving pleasure palace from the Alhambra, the Partal (which is attached to a slightly later building decorated with fragmentary frescoes of turbaned figures), was erected during the reign of Muhammad III (1302–9), while the summer palace of the Generalife, so famous for its gardens, probably dates back to the time of Ismail I (1314–25). As for the main Nasrid Palaces, with their ornamentation of unrivalled brilliance and complexity, these acquired their present appearance largely during the long reigns of Yusuf I (1333–54) and his successor Muhammad V (1354–91), when Granada entered what is usually known as its Golden Age.

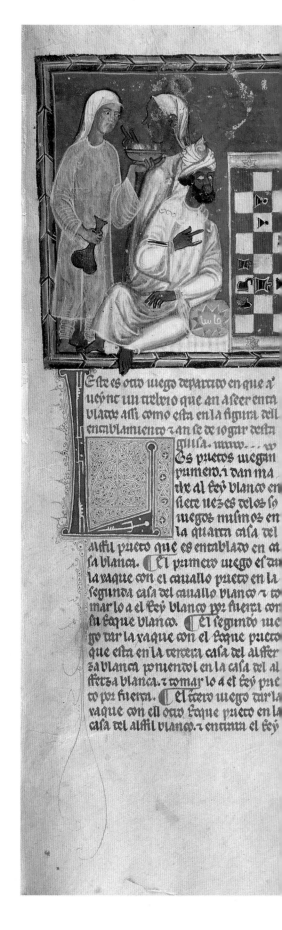

nco en la fegunda cafa de fu alffer
¶ El quarto mego tir la xaque
e ell alffil pueto en la quarta cafa
cauallo blanco.z entran el rey b.
nco en la tercera cafa te fu alffer
¶ El quinto mego tir la xaque
e el faque con el faque pueto en
cafa del alfferza blanca.z entran
rey blanco en la quarta cafa te fu
fil. caff ffe encubueffe con fu foq
nco.romaigelo ya con effe mifmo
que z tir lie xaque z alongarfie
mego tel madir. ¶ El fefeno ute
tir la xaque co el alffil pueto en
tercera cafa tel foque pueto.z en tan
el rey blanco. en la quarta cafa tel
fil pueto. ¶ El fereno mego tir la
que z madir con ell alfferza pueta
la tcera cafa tel cauallo pueto. En
tir mego no ba otro tepartamuento
to que fe tir el madir en cafa fena
ba.z efta es la figura tellentabla
tento.

Certainly this was the most stable and prosperous period in Granada's Nasrid history; but the term Golden Age, and the cultural glories associated with the reigns of Yusuf and Muhammad, should not blind one to the continuing vulnerability of a country caught between the Christians to the north and the Moroccans to the south.

The political situation of the time was marked by the struggle of these two powers to gain control over the Straits of Gibraltar. It is another of the many paradoxes of Nasrid Granada that the rule of one of its greatest leaders, Yusuf I, should be darkened so early on by the catastrophic defeat in 1340 of the combined forces of the Nasrids and the Merinids while fighting Alfonso XI outside the town of Tarifa. This was the worst set-back suffered by the Spanish Muslims since Las Navas de Tolosa.

Even the years of peace that allowed the arts to flourish in Granada from the 1350s onwards were brought about more by chance than by military or political brilliance. Islamic sources are tactfully silent about the plague that prevented the Castilian king from returning to the siege of Gibraltar in 1349, and about the further respite given to the Muslims by the outbreak of civil war in Castile.

Meanwhile conflicts and tensions among the Muslims themselves continued to be as bloody as ever, leading to the violent deaths of many of the protagonists of Granada's Golden Age, including Yusuf I, who was stabbed by a deranged black slave while at prayer in the city's Great Mosque. His successor, Muhammad V, who came to the throne at the age of sixteen, narrowly escaped a similar fate five years later, when one hundred conspirators managed to scale the Alhambra, take the royal palace by surprise and place on the throne Muhammad's half-brother, Ismail. Muhammad, in the Generalife at the time, tried to make his way back into the Alhambra but, realizing the dangers in time, fled to Almería and eventually took refuge with the Merinids in Morocco. Three years later he successfully reclaimed his throne, by which time Ismail had been killed and replaced by yet another Nasrid prince, whose head would end up being sent to Muhammad by the latter's unpredictable Christian ally Peter the Cruel of Castile.

It was with Muhammad's second reign that Granada's Golden Age reached its apogee, culminating with the construction of the Palace of the Lions, which brought the art and architecture of the Alhambra to a point of near unsurpassable intricacy. According to a theory proposed by the stimulating, if also much criticized, modern historian of the Alhambra Oleg Grabar, Muhammad V's intention in greatly extending and embellishing the Nasrid Palaces was partly to turn the whole complex into a monument commemorating his successful taking of Algeciras from the Christians in 1379. If this is the case one can only reflect on the discrepancy between the glittering beauty of the architecture and the relative unimportance of the event it supposedly celebrates. The siege of Algeciras, though the greatest victory in the history of Granada's Golden Age, was of only short-term significance, for, barely

Chess was one of the more popular diversions at the court of the Nasrid rulers. This scene is from a treatise on chess and other board games translated from the Arabic by Alfonso the Wise.

This Christian *scriptorium*, as depicted
in an early 13th-century Mozarabic
manuscript, portrays the sort of writing
and copying duties carried out in the
Moorish institution known as the
Diwan al-insha.

ten years later, Muhammad V, realizing that he would be unable to keep the town permanently, withdrew his troops and left the place in ruins.

The insecurities of Golden Age Granada, and the contrast between the brilliance of its image and its often inglorious reality, are nowhere more apparent than in the lives of the poets and statesmen Ibn al-Khatib and Ibn Zamrak, who, after the sultans themselves, ranked as the two most important people of their time. Their lives are worth looking into in some detail, for they furnish much of the colourful human anecdote so necessary for a more realistic appreciation of what the Alhambra was like in its heyday.

Ibn al-Khatib, of Córdoban origin, was born in 1313 in the town of Loja, which guards the western entrance to Granada's fertile valley or *vega*. After losing both a brother and his father at the Battle of Tarifa of 1340, he was invited by Yusuf I to occupy the post of secretary in an institution known as the Diwan al-insha. This office, founded by Muhammad II as the Nasrid government's Department of Correspondence, had gradually taken on tasks less prosaic than the mere copying and drafting of documents. By Ibn al-Khatib's day it seems to have been the centre of local literary life and to have played a key role in the artistic evolution of the Alhambra, the decoration of which demanded the use of ever more complex and extensive calligraphy.

As well as being a poet whose works appeared on the Alhambra's walls, Ibn al-Khatib wrote prolifically on subjects ranging from music to medicine, compiled the most detailed account ever written on medieval Granada, and rose quickly to the post of vizier, which was the highest position in the Nasrid bureaucracy and entailed amongst its duties the directorship of the Diwan al-insha. The wealth he accumulated, and the extent of his influence at the court, would also inevitably be the source of enormous jealousy, which would eventually lead to exile and a brutal death.

His first taste of exile came after 1359, when he followed the deposed Muhammad V to Morocco, where, wishing perhaps to meditate on his fate, he went to Aghmat to visit the tomb of the most famous Spanish exile of them all, the Sevillian poet-king al-Mutamid. Interestingly, on his way there he seems to have acquired a manuscript containing the memoirs of the Zirid king 'Abd Allah.

With Muhammad V's reinstatement in Granada in 1362, Ibn al-Khatib also returned to Spain, but soon began to be concerned both by the future of al-Andalus and by the ever more paranoid behaviour of the sultan, whose suspicions against him were undoubtedly stoked by the up-and-coming poet Ibn Zamrak. In 1371, when news reached Granada that Ibn al-Khatib had fled from Gibraltar to Ceuta, and was meeting the Merinid sultan Abd al-Aziz, Ibn Zamrak, already a secretary at the Diwan al-insha, was appointed vizier in his place.

Though the career and ultimate fate of Ibn Zamrak were to echo those of Ibn al-Khatib, Ibn Zamrak did not have the advantage of his rival's wealthy and intellectual background. He came instead from a poor and humble family, being born in 1333 to an iron-worker from the Albaicín. At an early age he killed his father with a blow to the head, if we believe the intemperate commentary scrawled all over a book of his poems by one of Ibn al-Khatib's sons. Elsewhere in this book, over a passage describing Ibn Zamrak as having been been brought up 'pure and chaste', the defacer added that 'this imbecile Ibn Zamrak, this appalling secretary . . . was a creature of the vilest breeding, of the most despicable character, and of a totally insipid appearance'.

With such a background and personality, Ibn Zamrak would have been unlikely to have gone far in life had he not been lucky enough to have been born shortly before Yusuf I founded in Granada one of Spain's earliest *madrasas*, which were collegiate institutions with bursaries for the poor. At Granada's *madrasa*, where he was among the first intakes of students, Ibn Zamrak enjoyed the protection of a preacher at the Alhambra's mosque, and was then introduced by him to Ibn al-Khatib, who nurtured his talents, his ambitions and his envy.

Ibn Zamrak never attained the range of learning displayed by his scholarly mentor, and was predictably accused of plagiarism by Ibn al-Khatib's son. Nonetheless his fame as a poet was equalled by no other writer of his time. It is his verse more than that of any of his contemporaries that can be found today covering the filigree surfaces of the Alhambra, turning the whole into what has sometimes been described as the most luxurious book of poems ever produced.

Ibn Zamrak's strong presence in the Alhambra partly compensates for the absence of any name to which the architecture and decoration of the palaces can be ascribed. His lyrical, panegyric lines, with their references to shining orbs, nuptial diadems, enfolding wonders, crystal fountains, full moons, rising suns and paradise gardens,

'The brilliance of your great deeds is shining at your door, which exhales the scent of happiness and jubilation.'

Ibn Zamrak, from the poem inscribed on the walls of the Court of the Myrtles.

A detail of the poem by Ibn Zamrak praising Muhammad V for his victory at Algeciras is inscribed within the north gallery of the Court of the Myrtles.

have provided the basis for numerous romantic evocations of an Alhambra completely at variance with the sordid world of political manoeuvring in which the poet became so completely immersed during the second reign of Muhammad V.

The viciousness with which Ibn Zamrak began to pursue Ibn al-Khatib was remarkable, especially in view of all the help the elder poet had given him at the outset of his career. He accused Ibn al-Khatib of heresy and treason, provoking his flight to Morocco in 1371, and then became actively involved in attempts to have him extradited back to Spain. Moroccan laws of hospitality prevented this, but Ibn al-Khatib was nonetheless thrown into prison in Fez and forced to submit to trial at the hands of a Granadan delegation headed by Ibn Zamrak. Lengthy deliberations at the trial provoked the impatience of Ibn al-Khatib's enemies, who managed to have a group of henchmen force their way into the prison and strangle him. The poet was buried at a local cemetery, but his body was immediately removed from the tomb and burnt.

Ibn al-Khatib's family and supporters may have found some consolation in the miserable fate that overtook Ibn Zamrak himself. After the death of his patron Muhammad V in 1391, Ibn Zamrak wrote a brief eulogy to the latter's successor Yusuf II, but this failed to save his fall from favour, and eventual sacking as vizier on the grounds of rudeness, incompetence and lack of understanding of economic matters. One night, during the summer of 1392, the sultan's henchmen broke into his house while he was reading the Koran with his two children and servants. All of them were killed in the presence of the rest of the household.

The glamour and the bloody reality of Golden Age Granada, so powerfully evoked by the lives of Ibn al-Khatib and Ibn Zamrak, are also embodied in their respective writings: whereas the latter's poems convey all the hedonism and refinement that went into the making of the Alhambra, Ibn al-Khatib's prose history *The Shining Rays of the Full Moon* belies its poetic title with its detailed and not wholly uncritical descriptions of Granada and its people. These descriptions help to pull further into focus the world for which the Alhambra was created.

The Granada evoked by Ibn al-Khatib was like a microcosm of al-Andalus during its heyday – a place of dazzling ethnic diversity where people of Spanish origin mingled with people from every part of North Africa and the Near East. The vast majority were of course Muslims, but there were also significant communities of Jews and even of Catholics, the former numbering about 3,000 and distinguished by being forced to wear yellow breeches and no turbans, and the latter mainly comprising a mixture of merchants (particularly from Catalonia and Genoa) and slaves. The varied make-up of Granada became ever more pronounced with the arrival of those escaping the Christian Reconquest, the first immigrants being principally from Valencia, Murcia and the northern Andalucían town of Baeza, the later ones from Córdoba, then Seville, and finally Jaén, Murcia and Antequera.

As early as 1311, Aragonese envoys to Pope Clement XI claimed that the city of Granada had no fewer than 200,000 inhabitants, a figure that had been obviously exaggerated to impress upon the Pope the glory that would be obtained from conquering the place. However, even though the actual figure probably amounted by Ibn al-Khatib's day to about a quarter of this claim (the size of the entire emirate at the end of the 15th century would have been no more than 300,000 inhabitants), Granada was still one of the most densely populated cities in Europe.

Within this large and diverse population Ibn al-Khatib was able to single out a number of distinctive Granadan characteristics, including a tendency to be proud and obstinate during arguments, and an Arabic speech that was 'heavily spiced with localisms and marked by lapses into long-windedness'. In terms of appearance, he described the Granadans as being 'physically pleasing', neither 'too short nor too tall . . . and endowed with medium-sized noses, clear skin, and for the most part black hair'. Though sporting clothes that in winter had colours corresponding to the wearer's 'wealth and status', they tended in the warmer months to 'affect garments of the most expensive striped Persian linen, silk, cotton or mohair, African jellabas, and Tunisian chiffon so fine that veils made of it must be worn doubled'; he likened the sight in summer of worshippers gathered at a mosque to 'a field of flowers on a pleasant spring day'.

Ibn al-Khatib appears initially to have lost all pretence at objectivity when evoking the lovely and heavily bejewelled women of Granada, whom he praised for 'being moderately plump with firm, voluptuous curves and long, sleek hair', for having 'sweet-smelling breath' and 'fresh-scented perfumes', and for 'moving with grace, and speaking with elegance, charm and wit'. However, he gave these idealized women a more human shape by criticizing them for 'reaching the extreme limits of what can be achieved in the arts of toilette and coiffure', for 'vying with one another in

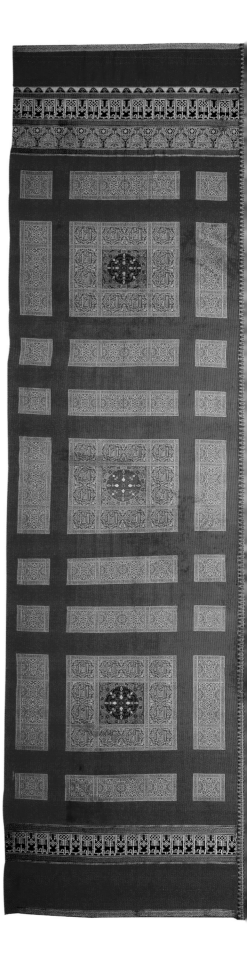

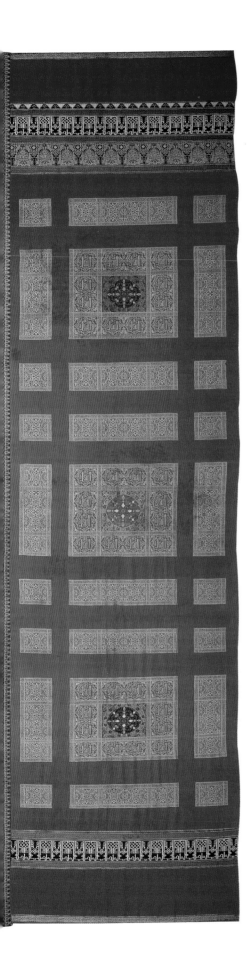

lavish displays of embroidered cloth-of-gold and brocade and other alluring finery', and, in short, for 'carrying luxurious fashions to the point of lunacy'. What he did not mention was that these women, though living in a city which he stressed as being very orthodox in its religious beliefs, enjoyed a degree of freedom that would have been unheard of in other Islamic countries: they were even to be seen mixing publicly with men in some of the poorer districts.

Accounts by Ibn al-Khatib and other early eyewitnesses also enable one to flesh out today's fragmentary survivals from medieval Granada and to recreate mentally what the city was like during its Islamic heyday. As with present-day Fez and other Moroccan cities, it was a congested labyrinth divided up not simply into the central medina and surrounding suburbs or *arbad*, but into a network of smaller quarters often associated with particular crafts guilds. Some of these areas were closed at night with their own gates; and most of them had either a mosque or an oratory, a bakery or communal oven, and a caravanserai, in the courtyard of which travelling merchants could sell their wares. Nearly all the streets, apart from the main ones, came to a dead end after weaving their way around houses and through arches; at times they were so narrow that two mules could not pass each other.

Urbanization was at its densest within the medina, in the middle of which stood the Great Mosque, encased by a maze of shops whose memory is recalled today in the daily market that extends up to the western and northern sides of the cathedral. Adjoining the building was Yusuf I's *madrasa*, the mosque of which has been preserved up to this day, hidden within a university building founded in the Renaissance.

Behind this extended the walled rectangular grid of streets constituting the market area of the Alcaicería, which was effectively a miniature city within the medina. It was divided up rigidly into three main zones: one was for money-changers and lenders, another for vendors of wool, mohair and cotton, and a third for those dealing in Islamic Granada's most famed and lucrative commodity – silk (the local silk industry, established by the Muslims in the mountainous district of the Alpujarras, was renowned all over Europe). The Alcaicería, with its special administrative set-up which was retained well into the Christian period, survived intact until 1843, when it was destroyed by fire. At the end of the 19th century it was replaced by a Moorish pastiche which, though filled today with shops selling trinkets and tourist souvenirs, still manages to suggest something of the district's past – an illusion strengthened by the distant view of the early 14th-century Casa del Carbón, the only surviving example anywhere in Europe of a medieval wheat exchange.

LEFT An example of one of the works that brought renown to Granada's silk industry, this exquisite 15th-century curtain, containing the Nasrid motto, 'There is no conqueror but God', is exactly the type of hanging that once decorated the walls of the Nasrid Palaces.

OVERLEAF Named by the Christians the Casa del Carbón after the charcoal merchants who lodged in it after 1492, this much restored early 14th-century structure served in Moorish times as a wheat exchange. The impressive entrance arch, with its Koranic inscription in praise of God, leads into the simple, three-storeyed courtyard where the merchants stayed and exhibited their wares.

The suburbs of Granada, more spacious in their layout than the medina, and dotted with trees and private gardens, grew up with the successive waves of immigrants from different parts of Spain, and were named either after the towns from which the new settlers had come or after professions common to the districts.

The Albaicín, the most luxurious of these suburbs, was populated initially by refugees from Baeza, but probably derived its name not from this but from the presence here of falconers. This quiet, white-walled district has kept more of its original Islamic aspect today than any other part of Granada, and provides an appropriate background to those wishing to indulge in oriental reveries while staring out across the Darro from the balconies of the Alhambra. Fortunately spared by the late 19th-century building fury that devastated the former medina, the Albaicín has nonetheless been altered by the widening of many of its tiny alleys for car access, and by the inexcusable demolition, continuing right up to recent times, of most of its genuine Islamic houses.

Of the Albaicín's public buildings, the most remarkable was perhaps the Maristan, a hospital created by Muhammad V in fulfilment of Islam's enlightened policy of offering scientific treatment for the insane. This building, within yards of the public thermal baths known now as the Bañuelo, was pulled down by Granada's civic authorities in 1843. All that survives is its foundation stone in today's Alhambra Museum, together with the two stone lion fountains that once discharged water first into the Maristan's pool and then into that of the Alhambra's Palace of the Partal.

The rest of the Albaicín was famed principally for the splendour of its private homes. Even in a city where the most modest and outwardly decrepit houses were known for being spotlessly clean inside and invariably served by running water, these were still deserving of special praise. The historian Bermúdez de Pedraza, describing the Albaicín at the beginning of the 17th century, wrote how this district's 'delightful' homes were richly 'embellished with damascene work', and had courtyards and orchards that were 'beautified by pools and the splashing water of fountains'.

It was above all the Islamic obsession with water that gave to Granada the idyllic aspect so commented on by early travellers. The obsession was driven both by a belief in the physical and spiritual benefits of water, and by an awareness of how water and the vegetation dependent on it signified luxury and prosperity. Consequently gardens with fountains and pools proliferated, not just in suburbs such as the Albaicín but also in the city's outskirts, which were soon covered with farms and Roman-style working villas. These outlying settlements made Ibn al-Khatib liken Granada to a mother surrounded by her children, and showed off to the full an Islamic genius for irrigation. The *vega*, cultivated down to its smallest parcel of land, became a showcase for the many crops that the Muslims had introduced to Spain, from figs, peaches, almonds and citrus fruit to cotton, hemp, flax and sugar cane.

The Albaicín, seen here from one of the palace windows of the Alhambra, was originally the site of Granada's medina before being transformed under the Nasrids into a prosperous suburb. Taken over in later centuries by a large population of gypsies, it is now inhabited by a mixture of wealthy villa owners and a significant proportion of the city's Muslim immigrants and Islamic converts.

RIGHT The everyday life of Islamic Spain
is wonderfully evoked by some of the
Moorish baths to be found in Granada
and its province. The oldest of these are
the thermal baths outside the beautiful
small town of Alhama de Granada.
Renowned since Roman times, and later
much frequented by the Nasrid rulers,
they were blamed by the 15th-century
Christian chronicler Fernando del Pulgar
for producing in the local Moorish
population 'a certain softness in their
bodies, from which proceeded idleness
and other deceits and evil dealings'.
Though the baths at Alhama's present
spa hotel have been completely altered
in modern times, the Islamic cistern
from which water is channelled into
them has been remarkably preserved,
and is one of Spain's most haunting
Moorish sites. Resembling a mysterious,
submerged mosque, it is built in stone,
which suggests that it might date back
to the time of the Córdoban caliphate.

OVERLEAF Behind an insignificant-
looking house in Granada's Albaicín lie
the town's sole surviving public baths
from the Islamic period. Known as the
Bañuelo, this extensive and impressively
complete brick complex was built
probably in the late 11th century and
incorporates a number of stone capitals
of Roman and Visigothic origin.

ABOVE The gardens of the Generalife, as seen from the shaded terrace of one of the villas of the Albaicín.

OPPOSITE The grandest of the few remaining Islamic houses in the Albaicín is the mid 15th-century Palace of Daralhorra, which was saved from falling completely into ruins by Torres Balbas, one of the principal 20th-century restorers of the Alhambra. Deriving its name from the Arabic for 'The House of the Queen', it belonged to the Nasrid family, and was lived in by the mother of Granada's last sultan, Boabdil.

The celebrated Islamic traveller Ibn Battuta, who visited Granada during the reign of Yusuf I and was entertained for two days in a private garden frequented by poets, noted how the city was 'embraced on all sides by orchards, gardens, pastures, villas and vineyards'. Nearly two centuries later, when these environs were already showing the first signs of Christian neglect, the Venetian ambassador Andrea Navagiero was able to write of the *vega* that 'all of it is lovely, all extraordinarily pleasing to behold, all abounding in water . . . all full of trees bearing peaches of every kind, figs, quinces, apricots, sour cherries and so many other fruits that one can barely glimpse the sky for the density of the trees'.

Granada, which has so often been evoked in a way recalling Koranic descriptions of paradise, was certainly a paradise in the original, ancient Persian sense of an 'enclosed garden'. The city and its surroundings were like an enormous enclosed garden sheltering an endless succession of smaller such gardens. The private gardens of the Albaicín were versions in miniature of the greater walled complex of gardens that formed the Alhambra, which in turn was a microcosm of the mountain-enclosed *vega*. Viewed together these gardens created a truly celestial vision, as was conveyed by Ibn al-Khatib, who observed how 'the Alhambra, just like Granada itself, was so densely carpeted with green gardens that the clear coloured stone of its many tall towers shone amidst the dark greenery like the most brilliant of stars in the midst of an evening sky'.

Yet, as the fundamentally realistic Ibn al-Khatib might have pointed out himself, the walls of an enclosed garden have connotations as well of defensiveness and isolation, and can be thought of as reminders of the fragility of Granada's paradise. Beset for much of its history by a siege mentality, Islamic Granada was also a place whose very prosperity must be seen against such factors as the high taxes necessary for maintaining the annual tribute money to the Christians, the repeated devastation caused to the countryside by constant internal feuding, and the avarice and lack of brotherly help that Ibn al-Khatib found also to be characteristic of the Granadans.

The Golden Age of Granada, which had been less an era of cultural experimentation than one that had brilliantly re-elaborated Islamic achievements of the past, was destined to be of short duration. The beginnings of its sharp decline can conveniently be dated to the violent death in 1393 of Ibn Zamrak, whose image of Granada as a beautiful young bride crowned by the radiant head-dress of the Alhambra had given to this age a poetic perfection that would never again be recaptured. Problems in the Alhambra's chronology should make one wary of rigid claims about the monument's declining artistic standards from the 1390s onwards (the evidence has usually been found in the Torre de las Infantas, which is now thought to be earlier than was previously supposed). However, what cannot be overlooked is the fact that while diminished funds certainly precluded significant

additions to the complex in the 15th century, they also saved the existing palaces from being replaced by others, as might well have happened had the Nasrid fortunes continued to rise.

The last century of Nasrid rule in Granada was marked by desperation. The local coinage was debased as internecine feuding increased dramatically, above all as a result of the serious threat to Nasrid rule posed by the Abencerrages, whose rebelliousness would later fuel the imaginations of romantics such as Chateaubriand. Worse still, in trying to resolve these problems, the Nasrids could no longer depend to such an extent as before on the support of other Muslims. Instead they were now largely at the mercy of the ever more wary and unreliable Christians. Increasingly they were isolated from the rest of the Islamic world, which, with the rise of Tamerlane in the late 14th century, had shifted its seat of power from the Near East to Iran and central Asia. Unable to find a helpful ally in the by now greatly weakened Merinids in Morocco, the Nasrids turned for support first to Egypt, and then to the Ottoman Empire, but in vain. They had to rely purely on themselves and on their own ineffectual navy when, in 1462, the Christians laid siege to Gibraltar once again, and succeeded this time in capturing what was known to some Muslims as the 'Citadel of Islam'.

Three years after the loss of Gibraltar an Arab traveller visited Granada and wrote of the city that 'it is a meeting-place of illustrious people, poets, scientists, artists; there are here some of the finest men of our time, grandiose monuments, charming little corners ... with its Alhambra it is one of the great cities of Islam'. This rather exaggerated account, more descriptive of Granada's past than of its present, seems to have been influenced by an awareness of the city's potential imminent demise, for, he added with a sigh, 'the infidels are close at hand, and have taken the greater part of this land of al-Andalus'.

The year when this was written saw the accession to the throne of Granada's penultimate ruler, Abul-Hasan, whose life (like that of his son Boabdil) would be embellished by a number of romantic stories, invented presumably so as to try to add a certain lustre to the disastrous events of his unpopular reign. Prominent among these stories was that of his abandonment of his nobly bred wife Aisa for the beautiful Christian captive Isabel de Solís, which added a glamorous dimension to the unattractive family feuding that would soon tear the Nasrid family apart.

Unquestionably true, however, was the ominous fluke storm that devastated Granada in April 1478, in the midst of a massive military parade organized by Abul-Hasan as a demonstration of the strength of his army. Flooding and mudslides destroyed bridges and buildings, and put an additional strain on the country's finances, to which the sultan responded by increasing taxes and retrenching on military expenditure.

Granada was still recovering from this tragedy, with the sultan reputedly trying to forget his troubles in the company of 'dancing-girls', when, in 1469, the thrones of Aragón and Castile were united with the marriage of the Catholic monarchs Ferdinand and Isabella. The prospect of a united Spain was at last within grasp, and the long-threatened campaign against Granada more likely than ever.

OPPOSITE The Battle of La Higueruela (1417), a battle predating the full-scale Christian Reconquest of Granada by many years, is represented in a huge and intricately detailed fresco painted for the palace monastery of the Escorial in 1587. In the detail here the artist has taken the liberty of depicting the Christians fighting below the walls of Granada.

BELOW Ferdinand and Isabella, the creators of a united Christian Spain, in one of the few known likenesses executed during their lifetime.

ABOVE The view from Alhama de Granada down into the spectacular gorge that once contributed so greatly to the town's impregnable reputation.

OPPOSITE After the Christians captured the important town of Alcalá la Real in 1346, the Muslims relied heavily on the citadel of Moclín for defending Granada from the north. Referred to by Ferdinand V as the 'key to the *vega*', the citadel has retained its imposing ring of Nasrid walls, which remained in Muslim hands up to 1486. The former mosque in the lower half of the citadel was later transformed into a church, which today contains a much venerated image of Christ.

This campaign was finally launched in 1482 when a contingent led by the Christian commander Rodrigo Ponce de León managed surreptitiously to advance right into the heart of Granadan territory. After a bloody siege, they captured the supposedly impregnable town of Alhama de Granada, an enormously wealthy place much favoured by Granada's sultans on account of its thermal baths. Abul-Hasan arrived at the scene in time to see piles of corpses being devoured by carrion crows and dogs. He had the dogs killed ('not even the town's dogs could remain alive', commented one eyewitness), and attempted to regain his beloved Alhama, but eventually had to give up after the arrival of Christian reinforcements and the subsequent news of a large Christian army advancing towards Loja.

The Wars of Granada, depicted in exquisite detail in the choir stalls of Toledo Cathedral, and celebrated at their conclusion by the ringing of bells all over Europe, have often been imagined as a heroic, chivalrous struggle. In fact, they represented an anti-climactic, confused and unworthy ending to seven centuries of Islamic rule in Spain. The Christians, though routed at first at Loja, had relatively little difficulty in reconquering the emirate, thanks to a large extent to the deepening divisions within the Muslim side, and, in particular, to the duplicity of Boabdil, who, profiting from his father's absence and fall from grace following the loss of Alhama, used the support of the Abencerrages to install himself as Muhammad XII at Granada. Abul-Hasan, meanwhile, fled to Málaga, where, together with his bellicose brother Muhammad al-Zaghal (who himself had designs on the throne), tried to regain his authority by fighting back the Christians in the coastal district of the Axarquía. Boabdil, determined not to be outdone by his father and uncle, launched an offensive in 1483 against the Christians in Córdoba, but was almost immediately taken prisoner.

The grave split within the Nasrid camp was fully exploited by the Christians, who, after the capture of Boabdil in 1483, decided that their interests would be best served by releasing him immediately and setting him up as puppet emir in the town of Guadix, just to the east of Granada. Abul-Hasan died two years later, and was succeeded as sultan by al-Zaghal, who appealed to those radical Granadans bent solely on war. Boabdil, with the help of the Christians, was able to reach Granada and take over the Albaicín; but then, emulating the untrustworthy behaviour of his ancestor Muhammad I, appears to have switched allegiances shortly afterwards and made his peace with al-Zaghal.

It is not known for how long Boabdil remained a secret ally of the Christians, who, possibly infuriated by his ambivalent loyalties, embarked after 1489 on an all-out assault on the *vega*, winning in quick succession all its remaining towns save Granada itself. Al-Zaghal retreated to Almería before finally surrendering to the Christians on favourable terms and exiling himself to Africa. Boabdil, staying on in Granada to face a drawn-out siege, was soon secretly negotiating the inevitable surrender of his city.

Only three years after the taking of Granada in 1492, an artist of German origin, Rodrigo Aleman, carved in walnut in the choir of Toledo Cathedral numerous intricate scenes portraying all the stages of the conquest. Ferdinand and Isabella are seen here at the gates of Granada.

On 1 January 1492, a representative of Ferdinand and Isabella was admitted into the throne-room of the Alhambra, and given the keys to the palaces in exchange for a suitable written receipt. The following day, with the Christian flag already flying from the imposing watch tower of the Alcazaba, the ceremony of the handing over of the keys was repeated, this time for the benefit of the public, and with Boabdil kissing the hand of King Ferdinand. Boabdil, leaving the Alhambra by the gate known as that of the Seven Floors, is famously said to have turned around a short while later and burst into tears at the contemplation of what he had lost. Less well known is that the Catholic monarchs, on the day they took up residence in the Alhambra, were dressed in Islamic costume, thus bringing to a full circle the history of a palace city whose first Nasrid occupants had been attired as Christians.

This detail of costume, though seemingly insignificant, highlights the complexities of a period that has so often been perceived in the most crude black-and-white terms. While Catholic Granada continues to this day to celebrate every year the anniversary of the taking of the Alhambra, most visitors to the monument persist in the delusion that Boabdil's loss of the place was tantamount to being expelled from paradise, and that the Reconquest of Granada signified a sea-change that turned Spain almost overnight from a country bathed in light to one grovelling in darkness (to borrow an image used in 1893 by S. Lane-Poole in his sentimental book *The Moors in Spain*).

Over 100 years of cultural and political decline, and more than two and a half centuries of nominal subservience to Spain's Christian leaders helped ensure that the transition from Muslim to Christian Granada was not as abrupt as it might have been. Indeed the Muslims who decided to remain in Granada after 1492 were not at first significantly much worse off than they had been immediately before the conquest. Despite being segregated from the Christians and prevented from living in the Alhambra, they were able to practise their own customs and religion openly, and to do so in an environment free of the debilitating feuding that had characterized the last years of Nasrid rule. In comparison to the fate reserved by the Catholic monarchs for Spain's Jews and 'false converts', the Muslims might well have thought at first that they had got off lightly.

They would not of course continue to think so after 1499, following the appointment of Cardinal Cisneros as Archbishop of Granada, whose fanatical beliefs were in stark contrast to those of his predecessor, the first Archbishop of Granada, Fray Hernando de Talavera. Talavera believed that the Muslims would gradually assimilate Christianity, and should not have the religion forced upon them. Cisneros, completely reneging on an agreement reached between Boabdil and the Catholic monarchs, ordered the baptism of 60,000 Muslims, and organized a massive bonfire of Muslim books and manuscripts on Granada's Plaza de Bibarrambla – an act of cultural vandalism unsurpassed in Spanish history.

The Muslim uprising that was immediately and inevitably sparked off by this act spread from the isolated villages of the Alpujarras to all parts of eastern Andalucía, and was not finally suppressed until as late as 1501. Thereafter the lot of Spain's Muslims (or Moriscos, as they were now known) became even worse: they were obliged either to convert or to leave the country, and were forced to wear Christian clothes and speak in Spanish. The bishops' summary edict was largely ignored, and most of the Moriscos continued to practise their religion. Nonetheless the harsh way they had been treated shocked the sensibilities of tolerant foreign visitors such as the Italian Navagiero.

This scene from a late 16th-century ecclesiastical history of Granada shows the enforced baptism of the town's Moriscos on the orders of Cardinal Cisneros.

And yet, for all this brutal persecution of the Moriscos, there is indisputable evidence of a deep respect among the Christians for the Islamic culture they were publicly trying to negate. The Islamic practice of bathing was widely adopted by the Christians, despite being condemned by their priests as being conducive to moral turpitude and physical enfeeblement; and in 1502, while the Moriscos were being told to abandon their traditional clothes, King Ferdinand and his entourage were recorded as being 'dressed in Moorish style' – a style favoured by many other nobles, to judge from wardrobe inventories of the time. The Christians, furthermore, happily inherited from the Moriscos elements of their administrative system (for instance, in Granada's Alcaicería), learnt the silk trade from them, came to eat much the same food and even took up the strange Islamic habit of nibbling at pieces of porcelain.

But perhaps the most striking contradiction of this period is the fascination that the Catholic monarchs and their successors had for the Alhambra. Writers on the palace city from the Romantic period onwards, while acknowledging this enduring interest, have rarely been generous enough to state that without the Christian Reconquest of Granada the Alhambra would probably have gone the way of all the other medieval palaces of the Islamic world, and been either superseded by later structures or left to decay.

The desire of the Catholic monarchs to preserve the Alhambra might partly be explained in terms of their wanting to hand down to posterity a fine and curious example of the civilization they had conquered. But their interest in the place seems also to have stemmed from a genuine love of living there, which would be inherited by their daughter Joan the Mad. Naturally they made changes to meet their particular tastes and requirements; but their main contribution was to restore the parts that had been neglected by the last Nasrid rulers, and to do so with the aid of Morisco craftsmen whose work was virtually indistinguishable from that of their ancestors. These workmen proved indispensable as restorers after 1522, when an earthquake caused considerable damage in the western end of the palace complex – a disaster that might have provoked less sympathetic rulers of the Alhambra into having the place totally rebuilt in a modern, Christian style.

The threat of such a drastic reconstruction only began to loom large in 1526, when the grandson of the Catholic monarchs, Charles V, came to the Alhambra on his honeymoon with Isabel of Portugal. His initial response to the place was fortunately so enthusiastic that he is said to have sighed, 'Ill-fated was the man who lost all this!' Unhappily, however, this was not an emotion shared either by his courtiers – who complained bitterly about the lodgings assigned to them – or by his queen, who on seeing her intended bedroom is said to have rushed off with her retinue down to a convent in the lower town.

The modern luxuries to which Charles's court had become accustomed must have made the Alhambra seem woefully old-fashioned and uncomfortable. But there was also a fundamental problem about the architecture that has often been glossed over by the romantically inclined: a structure so open to the elements and incorporating so many pools and fountains might be all very well for the summer, but would have been rather less inviting during Granada's cold and damp winters. Moreover, as Charles soon realized, it was a building wholly unsuitable for Renaissance court ceremonial, on which the business of government depended.

Charles V, determined to make Granada the symbolic capital of the new Spain, was more or less obliged to build a new palace. However, it is unlikely that he ever seriously considered doing so by pulling down the palaces of his Muslim predecessors. His mother and his grandparents urged him not to do so, and he had recently visited Córdoba and been horrified by the cathedral built on his authority within the town's Great Mosque, which he said had destroyed 'what was unique in the world' for the sake of something that could be seen anywhere.

His chosen solution for the Alhambra was to allow a virtually untested Italian-trained architect, Pedro Machuca, to construct alongside the Nasrid Palaces a classical structure of dramatic scale and uncompromising geometrical boldness. Daringly original not just in a Spanish but also in a European context, Machuca's pioneering Renaissance building clashed with its setting in much the same way that the Pompidou Centre would do in Paris in the 1970s. This clash came to be seen by later

LEFT AND OVERLEAF The Palace of Charles V, one of the pioneering Renaissance structures in Europe, was begun in 1527 by an architect of apparently limited experience, Pedro Machuca. Machuca, who trained with Michelangelo in Italy up to 1520, came to the attention of Charles V through the intercession of the Alhambra's first governor, the Count of Tendilla, for whom he had served as a page. He supervised the construction of the building until his death in 1550, by which date the four façades had largely been built, as well as the walls of the circular patio. The work was taken over first by his son Luis and then by an architect who was in close consultation with the appropriately uncompromising and severe architect of the palace monastery of the Escorial, Juan de Herrera. However, the combination of the second Moorish uprising of 1568 and the declining interest in Granada shown by the Spanish monarchy led to the abandonment of the building in 1631.

The architecture of the palace, with its rigid symmetries, restrained ornament and massively rusticated exterior, is in every way unlike that of the Nasrid Palaces. The poet García Lorca famously referred to the stylistic clash between the two palaces in terms of 'the fatal duel that throbs in the heart of each of Granada's citizens'.

writers as a conflict between Christian brutality and Islamic sensitivity rather than as an acknowledgment on Machuca's part that the only way to compete with a work of Islamic genius was to produce a building more striking than any other Christian structure of the time.

In 1527, shortly after commissioning the palace from Machuca, Charles V left Granada, never to return. His subsequent military campaigns all over Europe, and his eventual abdication and retirement to a remote monastery in Extremadura, put an end to his plans to turn Granada into the permanent residence of the Spanish court. Without his energy and enthusiasm, work on the palace gradually slowed down, and was finally abandoned in 1631; the unfinished structure, intended originally as part of a grander scheme, would be left without a roof until as late as the 1960s. Though travellers to Granada from the 18th century onwards simultaneously bemoaned and revelled in the later neglected state of the Nasrid Palaces, few people confessed to finding a comparable poignancy in the incomplete Palace of Charles V, which, in its own way, was no less evocative of lost glory than the Islamic ruins alongside it.

Respect for the Nasrid achievements in the Alhambra would always be maintained by the Habsburg monarchs, even though relations between the Christians and the Moriscos continued to deteriorate. In 1568 another rebellion broke out, this time with Moriscos marching through the streets of the Albaicín and threatening to scale the Alhambra with rope ladders. The quelling of this revolt in 1571 had the immediate consequence of having the Moriscos banned from the former kingdom of Granada, and led eventually to the economically catastophic decision to have them expelled from Spain itself at the beginning of the 17th century. The unfortunate Moriscos, disparaged as Africans in Spain and as Spaniards in Africa, perpetuated in African towns as faraway as Timbuktu an art and architecture of distant Nasrid inspiration, and even associated themselves with districts that are still known to this day as 'Andalucían'. Craft traditions dating back to the great days of the Alhambra obstinately persist, as do rumours of keys to ancestral homes in Granada.

The coffered ceiling of the central colonnade was only added in the 1960s. Until then the columns had stood exposed to the sky like those of some ancient ruin.

The Alhambra itself, without the help of Moorish craftsmen to maintain and restore it, became more vulnerable than ever to damage and decay – a situation further exacerbated by the diminishing funds available for the upkeep of the buildings. Charles V had laid aside for this the annual tribute money that the Moriscos were still obliged to pay after 1492; but from 1571 onwards the Alhambra had to rely instead on money conceded by Philip II from the rent of sugar cane works near Seville, as well as on the revenue from the produce of a handful of Granadan estates. The insufficiency of these funds, combined with the lack of skilled restorers, became depressingly apparent after 1590, when a powder factory blew up in the Albaicín and sparked off a major fire in the Alhambra. The building would not be restored until many years later, by which time the only way of repairing one of the honeycombed ceilings in the Palace of the Lions was to replace it with a baroque one.

Much of the restoration work carried out in the Nasrid Palaces in the 17th century was done in preparation for the stay there of Philip IV in 1624. The money for this came mainly from Granada's municipal coffers; however, the military leaders in charge of the Alcazaba were obliged themselves to pay for the damage caused in 1616 by their having turned the Hall of the Ambassadors and the Court of the Myrtles into a store for arms and ammunition. Great sums of money were spent, but not, it appears, a sufficient amount to disguise the scale of what remained to be done. With the departure of Philip IV, the financially depressed city of Granada lost some of the willpower needed to maintain and continue restoring the Alhambra. The monument's fate was finally sealed in 1717, when the new Bourbon king, Philip V, abolished the post of governor, the last occupant of which, the Duke of Mondújar, had been a supporter of the Habsburgs in the Spanish Wars of Succession. Before departing with his large retinue of civil servants, the enraged duke took his revenge on the king by demolishing the governor's residence, a building considered by the German traveller Hieronymus Münzer in 1494 as the most beautiful of all the Alhambra's palaces. Gypsies and vagrants began moving in to the vacated site, and the Alhambra was soon reduced from a royal city to an impoverished community living among ruins. Within a remarkably short period of time memories of what the Nasrid Palaces had originally been like were largely forgotten, and travellers were forced increasingly to turn to their imaginations to try to bring new life to the abandoned halls and courtyards.

ABOVE In Girault de Prangey's view of the Hall of the Kings in 1833, vagrants listlessly stand guard over a section of broken floor littered with exquisite ornamental fragments.

OPPOSITE The full poignancy of the Alhambra's later neglect is captured by the British artist John Frederick Lewis in this sketch of 1833 depicting the richly ornamented façade of the Palace of Comares. This gives a good idea of the extent to which the stucco decorations of today are a modern replacement.

INSIDE THE LABYRINTH

A Tour of the Alhambra and the Generalife

Two views of one of the more secret corners of the Alhambra, now sadly
out of bounds to visitors. The gallery (*left*) was built in the 16th century to
join the Palace of the Lions to the once freestanding Peinador de la Reina, a
lantern tower converted by Charles V into a boudoir for Isabel of Portugal.
The tower is covered with fragments of Renaissance frescoes, and is
surrounded by a balcony with views towards the Generalife (*above*).

VISITORS TO THE ALHAMBRA inclined to reverie have often set off on a tour of the monument by trying to spirit themselves back to the glorious days of the Nasrids. Sadly for those hoping to enjoy these pleasant delusions, reality intervenes today in the form of a timed ticket that has to be purchased from a distant and singularly unattractive concrete building, from where the easiest approach to the Nasrid Palaces and the Alcazaba is either along a dull modern alley of cypresses, or else on the Disneyland-like attraction known as the Alhambra train.

Traditionally there were four main approaches to the Alhambra. The most direct one from the city of Granada was originally through the Puerta de las Armas, a gate attached to the Alcazaba, at the western end of the complex. This route, favoured in Nasrid times by townspeople coming to the Alhambra to pay their taxes, sort out their business problems or be granted an audience, is now closed to visitors and overgrown. The bosky and largely abandoned wilderness through which it passes recalls the poignant state of neglect which must have confronted travellers to the Alhambra in the 18th and early 19th centuries.

Still accessible to visitors, however, and wonderfully evocative, is the footpath known as the Cuesta de los Chinos. Its name, though conjuring up visions of Chinese ambassadors to

The neglected path (*above*) that climbs up into the now permanently closed Puerta de las Armas was once the principal approach to the Alhambra for those coming directly from the city. The gate, simpler in style and probably much earlier in date than the two principal ones on the Alhambra's southern walls, leads into the northern barbican of the Alcazaba (*right*). Rising in the background is the keep or Torre de la Guardia.

the Nasrid court, is derived from the local word for pebbles. Beginning its steep ascent from the outskirts of the Albaicín, this now little-used path runs between the northern walls of the Alhambra and the orchards of the Generalife before ending up today near the modern ticket office and car park. Originally it led to the Alhambra's easternmost gate, the Puerta del Arrabal. Right up to Christian times, this was a place for changing horses for those who had stayed overnight in the Alhambra and wished to leave without having to pass through Granada itself, where they would have been obliged to pay a traveller's tax.

The vast majority of civilian travellers to the Alhambra would have been put up in the district of workshops, lesser palaces and small domestic houses that comprised the medina, the main entrance to which was the gate of the Bab al-Ghadur, now almost wholly rebuilt, on the south-eastern side of the royal city. Though the Arabs prosaically named this gate after an adjoining water cistern, the Christians with great poetic licence came to refer to it as the 'Gate of the Seven Floors', presumably on account of its having once been crowned by a two-storeyed dwelling used by the

military commander who controlled the precinct. (One of these storeys had already fallen into ruins by 1815, when Napoleon's retreating troops decided to blow up the whole structure.) The monumentality of the gate made it a suitably majestic backdrop to the various jousts and military parades that are known to have been enacted on the esplanade in front of it, including Abul-Hasan's ominously ill-timed parade of 1473. Some people have even identified the gate as the mythical 'traitor's gate', where Boabdil publicly handed over the keys of the Alhambra to Ferdinand and Isabella in 1492.

An early variation of this myth is evident in a depiction of the same event (which probably took place outside a minor gate in the vicinity) in a carving of *c.*1520 in Granada Cathedral. The carving shows Boabdil giving up the keys underneath the Alhambra's most important gate after Granada started expanding southwards in the 1490s – the so-called Gate of Justice or Bab al-Shari'a.

Until the recent creation of the Alhambra's new ticket office, and the diversion of all car and coach traffic to an outlying ring road, tourists approached the royal city along the Cuesta de Gomélez, which climbs towards the Bab al-Shari'a from Granada's Plaza Nueva. After ascending between steep rows of houses this route passes under the Renaissance Puerta de las Granadas, where ragged gaps in the arch serve as reminders of the days when large tour buses were allowed to go through it.

The gate also gives the impression that you are about to enter an outer ring of walls encircling the Alhambra, whereas in fact you have merely reached the limits of the formerly walled township of Granada. An area of wooded parkland opens up beyond, covering the narrow valley that divides the main body of the Alhambra from the outlying towers of the Torres Bermejas. A rare example of an area of land near Granada that is much more wooded now than it was in Islamic times, this valley had been left largely bare by the Muslims for obvious defensive purposes, and was not extensively planted with trees until after the arrival of the French in 1812.

The presence of the wood prevents you from seeing, until you are almost at the foot of the Alhambra's southern walls, the towering and richly decorated Bab al-Shari'a, which projects its whole body outside the precinct wall to form the most impressive surviving fortress gate from Islamic Spain. The mood of mounting excitement felt by most travellers on approaching the Alhambra has generally been heightened by the sight of this superlative structure, where, by the early 19th century, there were usually posted two or three somnolent and bedraggled soldiers, together with a similarly unprepossessing local guide. So vulnerable were the sensibilities of newly arrived foreigners such as Washington Irving that even the soldiers, dozing on their stone benches, were transformed in their imagination into the 'successors of the Zegris and the Abencerrages'.

Impressionability of this sort was of course fully exploited by the guides, who, after securing the trust of travellers by insisting on being true 'sons of the Alhambra' (members of families who had lived here for centuries) went on to perpetuate the

The southern walls of the Alcazaba look out towards the Sierra Nevada across the exotic woodland planted by the French in the 19th century.

still commonly held delusion that the Bab al-Shari'a had been used by the Muslims as a court of justice. This delusion – caused by an early mistranslation that turned the Gate of the Esplanade into the Gate of Justice – led Théophile Gautier to reflect on how the sleeping soldiers were 'taking their siesta in the very place where the caliphs, seated on divans of gold brocade, their black eyes immobile in their marble faces, their fingers sunk in the waves of their silky beards, listened with a distracted and solemn air to the demands of the faithful'.

The imagination of visitors has been further fired by two enigmatic carvings above the gate's massive outer arch and the smaller inner one. The first of these symbols is an outstretched hand that has been variously interpreted as a lucky charm, a gesture of peace and a representation of the five fundamental precepts of Islam (namely belief in a single God and in his Servant and Prophet Muhammad, prayer, the giving of alms, fasting and pilgrimage to Mecca). The second carving, between the arch and an inscription recording that the gate was built by Yusuf I in 1348, is of a key. This motif is repeated above a number of other Granadan gates, and was believed by the great Christian commander Hurtado de Mendoza to have been part of the Nasrid family coat of arms. It has been more plausibly identified both as a symbol denoting entry into a city, and as a reference to the power conceded to Muhammad to open and close the gates of heaven. Inevitably a number of more obscure readings have been made, and local guides have even entertained the likes of Irving and Gautier by referring to a legend claiming that Granada would never be taken until

Known misleadingly since Christian times as the Gate of Justice (*below right*), the Bab al-Shari'a or Gate of the Esplanade is the grandest of the Alhambra's entrances as well as one of the greatest examples in Spain of Islamic military architecture. The man in charge of defending the battlements had quarters in the upper part of the tower, from where boiling oil and other objects were thrown on attackers who managed to get past the massive outer arch. The enigmatic carvings, on the outer and inner arches respectively, of an outstretched hand and a key (*below*), have always intrigued visitors; their exact meaning has been much debated.

the key had been grasped by the hand. In a rare moment of common sense, Gautier noted that though Granada was lost the two hieroglyphics had always remained firmly in place.

It is doubtful in any case whether the gate's symbolism, or indeed the exquisite polychrome decoration covering the lunette above the inner arch, would have been of absorbing interest to any advancing enemies, who, once past the outer, doorless arch, would have found themselves in a small space open to the sky, where boiling oil and other missiles would have been relentlessly hurled down on them. After managing to survive these attacks and to break down the heavy inner doors, they would then have had to negotiate the dark ramp that runs below the dwelling once occupied by the master of the gate. To make matters worse the ramp was turned back on itself, thus giving the gate's defenders a greater chance of blocking off the enemy.

Venturing through what Irving called this 'spell-bound gateway', the visitor finally arrives inside the Alhambra, and has only a short uphill walk before emerging near the now free-standing Puerta del Vino, which once stood on the boundary wall separating the district of the royal palaces from the area in front of the Alcazaba. This gate, dating back to *c.*1300 and named perhaps after the tax-free wine that was sold here after 1556, became the subject of a musical composition by Debussy that was described by his poet friend García Lorca as conveying 'all the emotional themes of the Granada night, the blue remoteness of the *vega*, the sierra greeting the tremulous Mediterranean, the enormous barbs of the clouds sunk into the distance, the admirable rubato of the city, the hallucinatory poetry of its underground waters'. Debussy never saw the gate, and wrote his *Puerta del Vino* purely from seeing a sepia postcard that would certainly not have given any idea of the structure's rich ceramic decoration and extensive fragments of polychromy. Most of the ornamentation is on the side facing the palaces, and is the legacy of Muhammad V, who had the gate remodelled as a triumphal arch honouring his victory at Algeciras in 1367, and – if the historian Oleg Grabar's theory is to be believed – might even have intended it as part of a grander commemorative scheme embracing the whole of his palatial domain.

Neither the decorative detailing nor the monument's important associations seem to be much appreciated by travellers, most of whom, by this stage of their visit to the Alhambra, are overcome by an overwhelming desire to set foot as soon as possible inside the Nasrid Palaces. In their haste to do so they tend also to neglect the remarkably well-preserved Alcazaba, which exemplifies not only the genius for military

The Puerta del Vino is the gate marking the entrance to the royal precinct of the Alhambra. Shown here is its outer side, which is more plainly decorated than the one facing the Nasrid Palaces. Though it bears an inscription in praise of Muhammad V, the gate dates back to the time of Muhammad II, and as such is the oldest part of the palace complex to survive.

architecture inherited by the Nasrids from the Almohads, but also the Islamic adoption of a highly evolved Roman system of urban planning.

To reach the Alcazaba from the Puerta del Vino you would originally have had to cross a small ravine. This was filled in by the Christians in 1494, when they built the cisterns that give this area its present name of Plaza de los Aljibes. The triangular-shaped citadel consists of a short outer walled precinct and a taller inner one that was largely the work of the Zirids. Dominating the eastern end is the keep or Torre del Homenaje, which was where the citadel's commander was lodged, in rooms possibly used beforehand by the founder of the Nasrid dynasty, Muhammad I. On the opposite end of the complex, rising above the precipitous western extremity of the hill, is the similarly austere watchtower or Torre de la Vela, which was crowned by the Christians first by a cross and then by a bell tower that is still sounded yearly to commemorate their taking of the Alhambra.

Between the two main towers of the Alcazaba extends what in all other known medieval fortresses would have been an empty space occupied only by tents and other makeshift structures that could easily be dismantled so as to allow more room for troops to manoeuvre in times of war. However, when the Alcazaba was integrated into the greater defensive system constituting the Alhambra itself, the inner square or Plaza de las Armas was turned into a miniature township complete with paved streets, residences for the army élite and – immediately below the Torre de la Vela – a public bath or *hammam* attached to the cistern built by Muhammad I.

The sophistication of this residential district was reflected in a remarkable plumbing and drainage system which brought in clean drinking water through ceramic tubes, and removed rain and dirty water in drains laid below the latrines in each house. The constant sounds of water from the Alcazaba were loud enough to be heard in the Nasrid Palaces, according to Ibn al-Khatib; and so fresh was the cistern's water, and so hygienic the plumbing, that water-carriers from Granada would still be coming here five centuries later to fill up their earthenware vessels.

Thanks to early 20th-century archaeological work which has left the foundations of the houses exposed, the Alcazaba is now the most fully excavated part of the Alhambra, and one of the few areas of the complex whose original character can be evoked with any degree of historical accuracy. Even the most obsessively scholarly of present-day students of the Alhambra, Antonio Fernández-Puertas, has allowed himself (in his recent monumental tome, *The Alhambra*) to interrupt his dense scientific prose to conjure up an Alcazaba of white-washed walls, flower-filled patios, women making their way to the *hammam*, children playing in the streets, candles flickering behind latticed windows, muezzins crying at dusk and nocturnal feasts echoing with plaintive music.

The western end of the Alcazaba is seen here from the Torres Bermejas, to which it is joined by the ruined wall visible in the left foreground. The belfry crowning the watch tower or Torre de la Vela was placed there in 1773, and was once used both to control the irrigation times of the *vega* and to alert the townspeople in times of danger.

Modern excavations exposed the small township comprising the Alcazaba's lozenge-shaped Plaza de las Armas (*above* and *opposite*), which was a residential area reserved for the military elite and their families. The keep shown here (*above*) is where the military commander lived.

Scenes such as these – which could have come from the pages of an Irving or a Gautier – would appear to confirm all the most idyllic notions of the Alhambra were it not for the evidence, also assessed by Fernández-Puertas, that immediately below this world of refinement and sanitary concern there existed a network of completely dark and unsanitized dungeons accessible only through the trapdoors on top of cone-shaped vaults. This was where Muhammad V's usurper, Ismail II, was strangled by his successor, Muhammad VI; and it was from these death-filled cells that the luckier of the Christian slaves were taken out by day to help the Nasrid rulers in the construction of their architectural dreams. 'You imposed chains on the captives, and dawn found them at your door, building your palaces as your servants,' reads a line of verse by Ibn Zamrak, inscribed on one of the walls of the celebrated Court of the Myrtles.

Imagining yourself not as a slave but as someone visiting the Alhambra either on business or as an emissary, you can now move on from the Alcazaba to the royal palaces by following in your mind the route used by those who had journeyed from Granada by way of the Puerta de las Armas. On the other side of this gate you would have come to the Alcazaba's northern barbican (the space between the two walled precincts), where, to ensure that you were not carrying any arms, you would have been obliged to proceed for ninety metres with your unprotected right hand in full view of the soldiers who were keeping a close watch on you from the top of the inner walls. At the end of the barbican, you would have had to pass through a further security control (situated at a gate tower later turned by the Christians into a rounded bastion) before finally leaving the Alcazaba and entering an area then taken up by a combination of a market and the improvised sleeping quarters of the less fortunate other ranks of the sultan's army.

From the time of Ismail I, the Alcazaba was directly linked to the the royal palaces by ramparts; but this did not stop the ordinary civilian from Granada from making his way as before across the market and up on to an esplanade that seems to have served as the palace forecourt (unearthed during excavations carried out in the 1950s). The entrance to the palace precinct was from a street that approached from the side and left the visitor in the part of the complex that would be the worst affected by 16th-century alterations and disasters. You would then have crossed two courtyards: the first, containing a small mosque added by Muhammad V, was entirely destroyed, but the second one survives, and is known today by the name of the Renaissance architect Pedro Machuca, who designed its sole remaining gallery and lived here while working on the Palace of Charles V. From what are now the fragments of an arched entrance in the Patio de Machuca's south-eastern corner, a stepped ascent led into the official room now known as the Mexuar, which was probably as far into the palace complex as most medieval visitors were allowed. Today it has become the starting point of a signposted itinerary around the buildings.

Before we can embark on this, we need fully to prepare ourselves for the shock of entering an artistic and architectural environment governed by rules and traditions with which most westerners are likely to be unfamiliar. The English traveller

A solitary Renaissance gallery set in modern gardens gives a very misleading impression of the once bustling public area that seems to have preceded the Nasrid Palaces. The gallery, known after its architect Pedro Machuca, is shown below bordered to the east by the rooms presumed to be the Mexuar or council chamber, behind which rises the imposing Tower of Comares. The so-called Patio de Machuca (*opposite*) is seen from inside the Mexuar, with the towers of the Alcazaba in the background.

James Pitt, attempting an artistic analysis of the monument as early as 1760, was honest enough to admit that 'words could not give an adequate idea of objects we are so little used to'. Nearly two centuries later, a group of Spanish architects, in a polemical publication entitled *The Alhambra Manifesto*, were still able to confess that the Alhambra was a monument that had rarely been looked at from an architect's point of view, not even by architects themselves, who, when faced with the Nasrid Palaces, merely reacted like ordinary tourists and let their responses be guided more by emotions than by the intellect.

Western expectations of what a palace should be like will be confounded by the Alhambra. For a start, the layout of the buildings is truly baffling, and has not been helped by Christian attempts at rationalization, which have resulted in the bringing together of what were originally at least two entirely separate palaces. The sense of disorientation likely to be felt by westerners was expressed by James Pitt, who noted with exasperation that 'it is impossible to lay down any plan of the Moorish Palace, as they [the architects] seem never to have taken more than one apartment into their idea at once', or to have spared any thought 'regarding the Communications, or symmetry of the whole'. Indeed, instead of symmetry, grand entrances, major focal points and a logical sequence of rooms, the visitor is confronted by a layout suggestive of secrecy and intrigue, with oblique and serpentine approaches to the innermost rooms, doors that give no obvious indication as to where they might lead, a maze of hidden passageways and corners, and a sense that with every step you take you are being furtively watched from behind latticed windows.

A further level of architectural complexity stems from the breakdown of the typical western barriers between exteriors and interiors. Miradors focus on surrounding gardens, rooms open up into landscaped courtyards and an abundance of water flows from open to enclosed spaces, echoing the sounds of rivers and softening in its reflections the hardness of man-made lines. Perhaps the most intellectually disconcerting, if also emotionally engaging, aspect of the palace architecture is the dissolution of the interior structure by an overall encrustation of rich and intricate ornament such as you would never suspect from the bare and humble-looking outer walls. 'The severe, simple, almost forbidding exterior of the Alhambra,' as the 19th-century traveller Richard Ford put it, 'gives no promise of the Aladdin gorgeousness which once shone within, when the opening of a single door, as if by the tap of a fairy's wand, admitted the stranger into an almost paradise.'

This 'Aladdin gorgeousness', though lacking today the former profusion of sumptuous carpets, curtains and silk hangings, the stained glass that once filled the windows, and most of the original polychromy, manages still to be so blinding in its

The Alhambra appears as a confusion of roofs when seen from the top of the complex's highest tower, the Tower of Comares. The view here is taken up almost entirely by the Palace of the Lions, which was once separated from the Palace of Comares by a narrow alley that ran directly below the roof seen here in the bottom right-hand corner. The unusual star-shaped tower in the upper background, crowning the Hall of the Abencerrages, is a reminder of the complex honeycombed dome to be found within.

opulence and so exotic in its forms that much time is needed before the dazzled western visitor will feel able to take in its individual components and try to make greater sense of the whole.

Especially intriguing is the geometrical complexity that made the Alhambra of absorbing interest to such a lover of visual paradox as the 20th-century illustrator M. C. Escher. This is present in the glazed and coloured tiles that cover the lower level of the walls. In their interlacing of abstract shapes (a technique of Persian origin), these create mesmerizing kaleidoscopic effects evoking at times both flickering stars and flowers bursting into bloom. Higher up, when the tiles give way to stucco, the ornamentation becomes more involved still, and gives to the walls a richness of design that was rightly compared by Ibn Zamrak (in an inscription in the so-called Room of the Two Sisters) to that of the finest of textiles.

Motifs of purely geometrical character vie on this upper level with the floral and vegetal ones known under the generic term of *ataurique*. This latter ornament, which was predominantly interpreted by the puritanical Almohads in terms of flat leaves, underwent a considerable transformation under the Nasrids. The original technique of carving directly into wet gesso was succeeded by the end of the 13th century by the use of moulds applied to plaster made up of powdered alabaster mixed with water. *Ataurique* forms increased in size, surface area, complexity and variety, and came also to be more extensively polychromed and to have a more refined finish. By the time of Muhammad V the *ataurique* was made, for the first time, to interlace with the strokes of the calligrapher, who reserved for these particular compositions the angular and stylized Kufic script (a more purely decorative and difficult to decipher alternative to the free-flowing Neskhi characters, the modern Arab script).

'This is a palace,' wrote the poet Ibn al-Yayyab on the walls of the Torre de la Cautiva, 'whose splendour is divided between its ceiling, its floor and its walls; the stucco and the tiles are true marvels, but the crafted wooden panels of the ceiling are yet more extraordinary.' In order to compete with the rest of a room's decoration sensational effects were indeed required for the ceilings, most of which were created out of a geometrical labyrinth of wooden panels that were carved, coloured and even occasionally covered with gesso on which stencilled floral motifs were then painted. More memorable still, however, and more special to the Alhambra, were those ceilings made up literally of thousands of the honeycomb forms known as *muqarnas*, which illustrate in spectacular fashion the extent to which the Muslim craftsmen were dependent on light – an element used here to provide the illusion of a sparkling and ever-changing celestial vision.

All this wealth of exotic ornament generally makes an unforgettable impression on visitors while at the same time leaving the frustrated sense of missing out on meanings that would have been more apparent had Islamic art been more figurative than decorative. Figurative scenes do in fact exist in the Alhambra, and Islam – contrary to what is generally thought – does not in itself necessarily ban their use, and prohibits only the representation of God and his prophet. However, the function

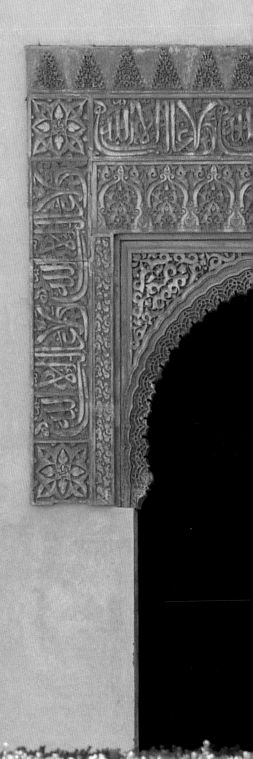

BELOW A burst of ornamental brilliance brings to life the otherwise relatively plain eastern side of the Court of the Myrtles.

OVERLEAF The Alhambra can easily
overwhelm visitors with the sheer
variety of its spaces, its profusion of
hidden corners and its staggering
range of intricate ornamental detail.

of images is taken on in the Alhambra, as in Islamic art generally, mainly by epigraphs, whose profusion here presents most westerners with the greatest barrier to the full artistic appreciation of the monument.

Of these epigraphs the most important in terms of meaning are the poems, which have an intimate relationship with their particular surroundings; but even the others, though comprising mainly a mixture of commemorative inscriptions and endless repetitions of Koranic incantations and the Nasrid motto 'The only conqueror is God!', indicate by their very dominance that the art of the Alhambra was looked at in its time in a very different and more meditative spirit than is generally possible today for a westerner.

For the medieval Islamic viewer the Alhambra's walls promised all the enjoyment to be had from leafing through an especially sumptuous book; but the experience of contemplating these walls, with all their monotonous-seeming repetition of forms and phrases, must also have been comparable to that of a fisherman staring at an expanse of apparently still but constantly moving water. The experience, of absorbing and mesmerizing interest for its original participants, has become irrecoverable for most of today's visitors, who can only, in the words of Ford, look with 'eyes that understand not'.

Unable today to view the art of the Nasrid Palaces with fully comprehending eyes, visitors might hope at least to be told something about the activities and events that took place within, and what each of the rooms was originally used for. Most travel books and local guides have duly obliged in this respect, but always with stories as fantastical as the romantic names significantly used to this day to identify all the rooms. The sad truth is that, in the almost total absence of contemporary accounts relating to the palaces, not to mention the survival *in situ* of any of the furniture, we have little from which to deduce the original function of most of the rooms other than the often enigmatic inscriptions on the walls. There is even the strong possibility that most of the rooms never had any fixed function in the first place, and that, as in many oriental interiors, the taking down or placing of a curtain or piece of furniture could transform a space into anything you needed it for at any given moment.

Unsettlingly, recent investigations into the palaces have succeeded mainly in questioning previously held theories, including most attempts to uncover in the buildings an overall logic in the planning. One of the more persistent of these earlier theories was that the Nasrid Palaces, in the form given to them under Muhammad V, were divided into three main areas representing a progression from the public, official world of the Mexuar, through to the courtly domain of the Hall of the Ambassadors, and on to the strictly private territory of the Palace of the Lions, where the sultan relaxed in the company of his harem and most intimate friends. Even today many of the visitors to the Nasrid Palaces continue to harbour notions of a reassuringly simple and logical progression as they embark in the Mexuar on the increasingly streamlined route mapped out for them by the Alhambra's present bureaucracy.

This route does not even begin on a note of certainty, for there is no absolute proof that the room now called the Mexuar was really the council chamber it is claimed to be. Few people doubt that this room and its surroundings formed an administrative and official zone preceding the palace proper; and there is also evidence from a 17th-century Spanish traveller through Muslim Africa that tribunals used to take place in entrance areas such as these. However, this part of the complex, dating back apparently to the time of Ismail I, suffered radical alterations in 1362, when Muhammad V held celebrations here in honour of the birth of the Prophet.

Today this room, with its confusing jumble of disparate elements (including a tile inscribed with the words 'Do not be afraid to ask for justice, for you will find it'), might or might not have been the place where citizens went to air grievances and requests before a council made up of the sultan's ministers and officials and even, on occasion, the sultan himself. If this was indeed the room's function it is certainly tempting to think of the four marble columns in the centre of the hall as denoting the former patio-like space where the council sat, under what was once a lantern whose stained-glass windows allowed the room to be penetrated by the 'Eye of God'.

In the 16th century, when rooms were added above the Mexuar to serve as quarters for the Alhambra's governors, the lantern was replaced by the present wooden ceiling. Additional changes were made when the hall was turned into a chapel by Charles V, who had the room extended by destroying a small courtyard to the north, but was at least respectful enough towards the Nasrids to have parts of the new structure decorated with tiles and stucco panels taken from elsewhere in the complex. Lines of praise to Allah were kept on the upper level of the walls, while below this Morisco craftsmen were commissioned to produce a magnificent tiled dado where, no less incongruously, the arms of the Nasrids were placed next to those of the Habsburgs and Cardinal Mendoza. During the 17th century the chapel was further embellished by the building at its northern end of a raised wooden choir, whose surviving gallery was described by Richard Ford as recalling 'the "beautifying and repairing" of some bungling churchwarden'.

Ford, like all his contemporaries, believed the Mexuar to have been a mosque, a delusion caused possibly by the presence behind the choir of an oratory, which, though accessible in his day by a modern opening, was originally an entirely separate structure that could be reached only from the Patio de Machuca. The oratory, one of the worst casualties of the explosion of 1590, and unreliably restored in 1917, has retained of its former decoration merely the inscription 'Do not be negligent. Come to Prayer.' But its most striking feature is the way it makes the most of the superb views over the Albaicín by having a row of arches forming a near continuous panoramic window. The openings were placed at what was once floor level, so that the panorama could be enjoyed by those praying in the obligatory squatting position; but Christian restorers, unaccustomed to this posture, lowered the floor for the benefit of westerners preferring to stand as they contemplated the view.

The Mexuar or council chamber, seen from its northern side, dominated by the raised wooden choir added in the 1630s when the room was converted into a chapel.

'Praise be given to God the only one;
Praise be given to God.
There is no power or strength but in God;
There is no God but God;
Muhammad is his messenger.'

Some of the inscribed lines from
the Koran to be found throughout
the Nasrid Palaces.

A modern opening connects the northern side of the Mexuar (*below*) with a much restored oratory (*right*), where the faithful once prayed before a stunning panorama of the Albaicín.

OVERLEAF Decorative details from the Mexuar, including the capital of one of the columns denoting the central space where the sultan and his council are thought to have sat.

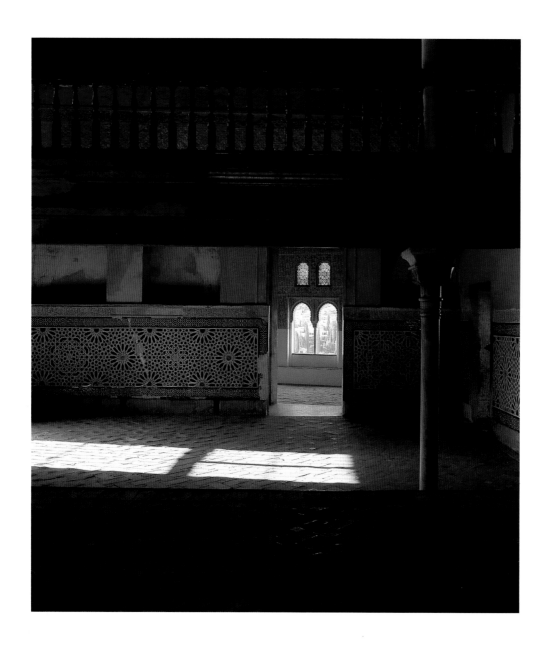

The area of the palace complex reserved for official meetings, trials and public audiences probably extended north-east of the Mexuar into the room known as the Cuarto Dorado, to which numerous changes were made (including the addition of a Gothic window bearing the heraldic symbols of the Catholic monarchs) after being turned into the private quarters of Ferdinand the Catholic's second wife, Germana de Foix. An arcaded portico on its southern side opens out into a courtyard, whose significance as a transitional zone between the public part of the complex and the sultan's actual residence was lost in later centuries, when it was left to decay to such an extent that it was even used for a short while as a

sheep pen and then as a poultry yard. Romantic travellers such as the English artist John Frederick Lewis, who memorably portrayed the courtyard in a drawing of 1833, must have enjoyed the poignant sensation of staring from the Cuarto Dorado to the magnificently ornamented wall opposite, which by then had crumbled away entirely in its lower half and had its upper storey partially hidden by a crudely placed wooden gallery. Nostalgic musings on past glories would doubtless have been more intense still had these travellers known that the wall they were looking at marked nothing less than the main entrance to the Nasrid Palaces.

Visitors have frequently commented on the Alhambra's apparent lack of a proper façade without realizing that this superb enclosed wall in the courtyard of the Cuarto Dorado was in fact intended as one. Built by Muhammad V one year after his victory at Algeciras in 1369, it is by far the most lavish of the Alhambra's exteriors, and must have been an appropriately splendid entrance to a domain out of bounds to most ordinary mortals.

Three steps raise the façade above the courtyard and lead to two doors surrounded by an inscription that testifies to the structure's royal status by quoting famous lines from the Koran which describe how Allah's throne 'comprises the heavens and earth'. Further up, above a row of latticed windows, a frieze of *muqarnas* support expansive and beautifully carved wooden eaves that crown the building both literally and symbolically, and also provide a convenient shade for the times when the sultan reputedly greeted his subjects from a seat placed between the two lower doors. A recent theory has it that with the creation of this façade the courtyard assumed the role of the Mexuar on those special occasions when the sultan's personal intercession was required to sort out a dispute or grant a favour. The grandeur and theatricality of the structure would certainly have conveyed an intimidating image of the sultan's power to those litigants and suppliants who humbly awaited an audience with him from the portico of the Cuarto Dorado.

As well as the usual lines from the Koran the palace façade has another inscription, probably by Ibn Zamrak, identifying the wall as a gate 'where roads split into two and the West thinks of itself as the East'. This enigmatic and slightly bewildering message points to the similarly mysterious anomaly, so typical of the teasing spirit of the Alhambra's layout, that those entering the palace have not one but two main

The small courtyard known as the Patio del Cuarto Dorado represented a transitional area between the administrative section of the royal precinct and the Palace of Comares proper. The magnificently ornamented southern side of the courtyard served as the palace's façade, as well as a probable backdrop to the sultan's public activities; seated between the two doors he would have been protected by the broad wooden eaves, which are the finest example of their kind in Islamic Spain. In Christian times the upper rooms of the Cuarto Dorado were used for a while as a residence for the Alhambra's governors.

OVERLEAF The Patio del Cuarto Dorado, *(left)*, which would be reduced by the early 19th century to a ruinous farmyard, is seen here from the Cuarto Dorado itself, a room off the northern side of the courtyard *(right)*. This was extensively remodelled during the time of Ferdinand and Isabella, as is evident from the central window, which has a strong late Gothic character.

doors from which to choose. The door on the right originally led nowhere and is imaginatively thought by some to have been put there with the intention of confusing potential assailants of the sultan.

Equally characteristic of the Alhambra is the discovery that the left-hand door leads obliquely into the palace, by way of a twisted ascending passageway that deposits visitors in the north-eastern corner of the palace's central courtyard, from which you approach the throne room in a comparably undramatic sideways fashion. It is not really surprising that such a circuitous unsignalled route was not to the tastes of a modern emperor such as Charles V, used as he was to grand entrances opening up on to grand staircases that directed his steps to the throne as surely as an altar leads the eye up the main aisle of a church.

From the Patio del Cuarto Dorado a dark passageway (*above*) climbs obliquely up to the Court of the Myrtles, passing on the way a tall niche where one of the sultan's guards would always have been stationed. This route emerges at the courtyard's north-western corner (*opposite*).

The building that you have so furtively entered is the earliest of the two main Nasrid Palaces, and is known as the Palace of Comares, a name said by the early 17th-century scholar Francisco Bermúdez de Pedraza to derive from the African town of Qumaris, from which, he claimed, the principal craftsmen employed by Yusuf I came; another, more recent, theory is that Comares is a derivative of the Arabic word *qamariyya*, which is used to describe the sort of coloured glass that once filled the windows of the throne room.

Etymological speculations, however, have been far from the minds of most first-time visitors to the palace, who, equally uncaring about the building's challenge to the demands of western ceremonial logic, have often likened the experience of emerging from the palace's dark entrance into its luminous central courtyard to a magical optical illusion. 'It seems,' wrote Gautier, echoing the view of thousands of travellers, 'that some enchanter's wand has transported you back to the Orient, some four or five centuries ago.'

The courtyard, referred to in the 16th century as the Patio de Comares, but usually celebrated since the Romantic era as the Court of the Myrtles, was thought until recently to have acquired its present form during the reign of Yusuf I, who inherited and possibly altered beyond recognition a structure begun by his father Ismail I. However, it has now been suggested that by the time of Yusuf's death all that had been fully completed of the future courtyard was the structural work on the narrow northern side, notably the imposing Tower of Comares, and the elegant seven-arched gallery in front of this. Muhammad V's workers, as well as finishing off the decoration of these areas (which included the placing in the gallery of yet another reference to his victory at Algeciras), seem also to have been responsible for turning what Yusuf might have left simply as an esplanade into a landscaped courtyard.

Plainly decorated structures with irregularly placed openings were erected on the two long sides of the courtyard, while a grander and more elaborate building

The Palace of Comares has as its centrepiece the so-called Court of the Myrtles, which is seen (*left*) from its narrow northern side, looking towards the part of the palace that was traditionally, and probably wrongly, thought to have been reserved for the Nasrid princes and their tutors. The long eastern side (*right*) with its small, irregularly spaced openings, is sometimes said to have been the women's quarters. The courtyard's galleries are highly decorated (*overleaf*).

went up on the southern side, which echoed the northern one only in having a gallery of seven arches. The creation in the middle of all this of the long central pool helped not only to cool and refresh the surrounding rooms, but also to dissolve all the courtyard's diverse and potentially discordant elements in a glittering surface where visitors could observe at night the shining of the stars and the moon, and enjoy by day the Matisse-like spectacle of gold fish swimming in between the reflected arches of the galleries.

The pool, with its two shallow fountains splashing lazily at either end, allows the mind to dream awhile before entering into the usual frustrating speculations about the function of each of the courtyard's different parts. A particular problem is posed by the building on the southern end, which was partly demolished at the back to accommodate one of the walls of the Palace of Charles V. The great indignation that was later caused by this so-called act of vandalism is probably out of all proportion to the damage that was actually done. Recent excavations under Machuca's palace uncovered little of structural significance, and thus strengthened the idea that the upper two storeys on the south side of the Court of the Myrtles were what they are today – covered and open passageways running along the back wall. The lack of evidence as to what might once have existed on the site has still not prevented writers from boldly stating either that the building was where the Nasrid princes and their tutors had their apartments, or even that this was an area shared by the sultan's concubines and the palace staff. There is a greater consensus of opinion as to the original function of the courtyard's plain and much altered side buildings. These, though partly used in Ford's day for the salting of fish, are generally supposed to have been the quarters of the sultan's permitted quota of four wives, who had narrow and windowless summer apartments on the lower level, and scarcely larger or more prepossessing winter ones above.

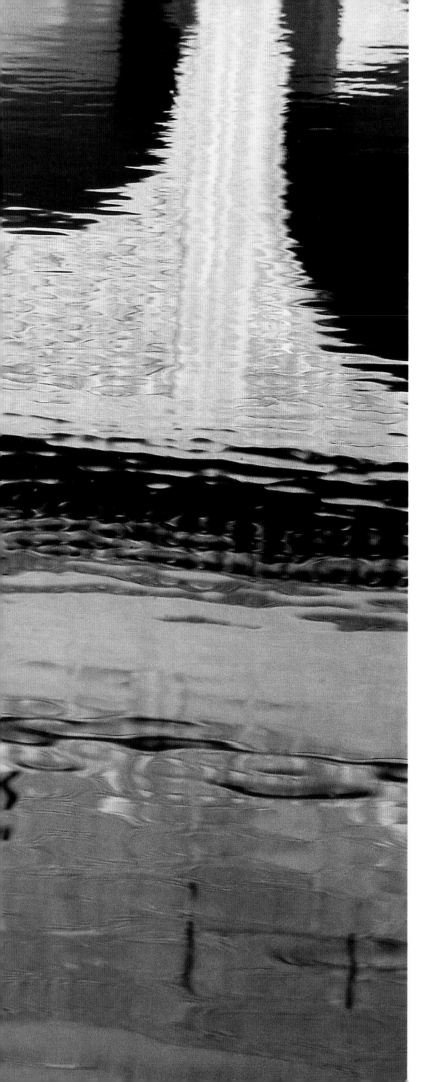

Ibn Zamrak, from an inscription on
the walls of the Nasrid Palaces.

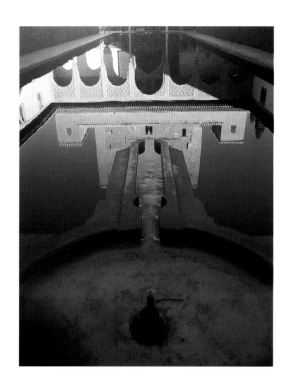

The Court of the Myrtles is dominated by a large pool,
which is shown here magically reflecting the imposing
Tower of Comares, and the gallery below it. Shallow
basins (*above*) feed the pool at its narrow ends.

ABOVE This monumental jar, once displayed near the entrance to the sultan's quarters in the Palace of Comares, is one of the finest surviving ceramics from Nasrid Spain. Though shaped like a traditional storage jar, it probably served a purely decorative function. Its combination of white, gold and blue appears to have been typical of Nasrid ceramics in general, to judge from other works now in the Alhambra Museum.

OPPOSITE The Sala de la Barca, which was probably used by the sultan as his summer bedroom, is seen here from the narrow arched space that leads into the throne room or Hall of the Ambassadors; in the background is the southern side of the Court of the Myrtles.

Everyone now is at least agreed that the sultan's quarters were inside the Tower of Comares, and that his daily activities and duties were all carried out around the northern end of the courtyard. Early 19th-century travellers, on the point of entering the tower, must have had their expectations raised yet further by the sight below the arches of the north gallery. The massive ceramic jar, now displayed more prosaically in the Alhambra Museum, is the sole surviving example in Spain of a type of ornamental jar that was once exported from Granada all over the Mediterranean. It gave early travellers a foretaste of the marvels beyond. Exemplifying the peaks of decorative sophistication attained by the Nasrids, it was crafted with astonishing intricacy in gold and blue, and inscribed with the words 'happiness and prosperity' – a sentiment hardly borne out by the fact that the vase used to be so badly looked after that a visitor was able to remove one of its handles.

A giant wooden door, a modern copy of one from the Palace of the Lions, takes the visitor from the north gallery into a part of the Alhambra described in 1832 by the French artist Girault de Prangey as having 'retained its magnificence and original nature better than any other'. Less than sixty years later a disastrous fire broke out next to the door, seriously charring the north gallery and destroying completely the first of the tower's rooms – the Sala de la Barca. This room, rebuilt entirely in 1967, probably derives its name from the repetition on the walls of the Arabic greeting *baraka*; but the word *barca* (meaning boat in Spanish) is also highly appropriate to the hull-like shape of the wooden ceiling, which floats on a foaming sea of *muqarnas*, and was praised by de Prangey as a 'marvellous cedarwood vault covered in drawings in bright and varied colours'.

Most visitors have assumed that the Sala de la Barca, preceding as it does the throne room, is merely an ante-chamber, whereas in fact it was probably the sultan's summer quarters, with the alcoves at either end being fitted out with divans and even a water closet. Christian courtiers, surprised at having to approach the throne room so obliquely, would have been even more shocked on discovering that they also had to cross – at least in the summer months – the sultan's bedroom.

The sultan's winter quarters were more discreetly situated in an upper room reached by a staircase off the secretive-looking passageway immediately beyond and to the left of the Sala de la Barca's inner arch (the passageway to the right led to a prayer niche or *mihrab*, which was later opened up by restorers who mistook it for a blocked door). Washington Irving, unaware that the sultan had slept in the upper part of the Tower of Comares (the highest of the Alhambra's towers), urged his readers to follow him up this same 'narrow, obscure and spiral staircase' all the way to the tower's battlements, where 'the proud monarchs of Granada and their queens have often ascended . . . to watch the approach of invading armies, or gaze with anxious hearts on the battles in the *vega*'.

Continuing from the Sala de la Barca into the throne room or Hall of the Ambassadors (which Irving implausibly claimed to have discovered by chance, after following the tower's dark staircase down to the bottom), Gautier could not help noticing in the jambs of the entrance arch two niches 'in sculpted white marble' that he believed to have been places where visitors to the room deposited their shoes

The throne room or Hall of the Ambassadors, the Alhambra's largest room, was where the sultan received foreign emissaries and other important visitors; it was also the place where the keys to the Alhambra were surrendered to the Christians on 1 January 1492. The sultan sat enthroned in front of the north wall's central window (*right*). His status as the spiritual as well as the temporal leader of his people was emphasized by the sumptuous wooden ceiling, which represents the seven heavens of the Islamic Paradise (*left*).

OVERLEAF The mysterious light that filters today through the windows of the throne room was once enhanced by stained glass.

out of deference to the sultan. The niches, ornamented not in marble but in stucco and ceramics, were in fact used for storing jugs of water. This is made clear in the surrounding poetic inscriptions, which have references respectively to the quenching of thirst and to the taking of visitors to an idyllic spot 'where the water is clean, fresh and of the purest sweetness'. Emissaries from afar, reaching the throne room after their long and dusty journeys, would certainly have appreciated the water, which was also a traditional Islamic symbol of

welcome. Great buckets of water, however, would have been necessary to bring back to their senses the thousands of over-emotional romantic travellers who suffered an almost literal delirium on seeing for the first time a hall filled with what de Prangey called 'the most stunning combination of forms, decoration and details that the imagination could ever create'.

The glance of medieval visitors would have been immediately directed towards the largest and most profusely ornamented of the three back windows, for this is where the sultan sat, his features obscured and made mysterious by the glow from the stained glass behind him. The space between him and those entering the room was partly protected by a central area of glazed floor tiles where no one was allowed to go because this would have involved walking over the name of God, which is in the inscribed words of the Nasrid motto (this indeed is the only known instance in Islamic art of the word 'God' being written on the floor).

Above the sultan's throne, and extending all the way to the top of this 18 m (60 ft) high room, soars a formerly multicoloured stucco 'tapestry' into which has been woven some of the richest sequences of geometrical motifs ever conceived in Islam, together with a dense landscape of *ataurique* and a wealth of panels with inscriptions ranging from lofty Koranic lines to the most lyrical of verses, and even to the odd piece of terse practical advice, such as 'Say only a few words, and you will leave in peace.' Crowning the hall, and giving emphasis to the notion of the sultan as the spiritual as well as the temporal leader of his people, is a ceiling employing no less than 8,017 pieces of wood to create a geometrical approximation of the heavens. Painted originally in seven different colours (as indicated on an inscribed tablet uncovered during recent restoration), the ceiling is arranged as seven concentric rings of stars representing the seven heavens of the Islamic Paradise, at the centre of which is the eighth and ultimate heaven that is God, whose presence is suggested in the central boss dripping with *muqarnas*. The whole is such a triumph of symbolism that even the ridges marking the changes of angle at which the ceiling is pitched have their own Koranic significance – they are the four rivers of Paradise.

'My master Yusuf,
the appointed of God,
has clothed me with a cloak
of glory and splendour
equal to no other.
And he has chosen me as
the throne of his kingdom.
May the greatness of this
throne be sustained by the
Lord who is enthroned
in heaven.'

Inscription from the throne room
of the Palace of Comares.

The throne room (*right* and *lower left*)
and adjoining Sala de la Barca (*centre
left* and *above left*) have always seduced
visitors with the intricacy of their
detailing and the extraordinary range
of their ornamental forms. The rope
barrier in the centre of the throne room
marks off a section of the floor laid
with ceramic tiles bearing the emblem,
'There is no conqueror but God.'

From the mystical heights of the throne room it was once but a short step to the pleasurable depths of the Turkish-style baths of the Comares *hammam*, which were accessible in Nasrid times by a door at the north-eastern corner of the Court of the Myrtles. Bathing in the Muslim world, as well as being an obligatory purification rite and a reflection of the Islamic obsession with personal hygiene, was also a major source of relaxation and entertainment. The baths were places where you could talk among friends and colleagues, soothe arthritic conditions and other bodily pains, and – in the case of women – eye up the bodies of prospective daughters-in-law.

The world of the Alhambra's baths is also one that need not tax too greatly the minds of modern visitors, who, for once during their tour of the Nasrid Palaces, do not have to concern themselves with hidden meanings or controversies about function. Built during the reigns of Ismail I and Yusuf I (an inscription referring to Muhammad V has proved to be a red herring placed by a 19th-century restorer), the baths continued to be used in Christian times, and are still very much as they once were, albeit heavily restored and with a garish coating of ceramic tiles installed in 1866. The main mental adjustment that has now to be made is to think of the original entrance as being from above – an approach that would have taken those descending from the Court of the Myrtles past the dwelling occupied by the guardian of the baths, who kept a rigorous watch on everyone coming in.

BELOW The Alhambra's baths were entered from the upper storey of the Sala de Camas. The first Christian governor, the Count of Tendilla, maintained that the sultan observed the naked women bathers from the balconies on this floor.

OPPOSITE The largest of the two hot rooms of the baths was partially heated by a *hypocaustum*; the star-shaped openings in the ceiling were intended to allow excess steam to escape and light to come in.

The guardian lived off the upper level of the Sala de Camas (literally the 'Hall of Beds'), a tall, lantern-lit space comparable in design to the original central area of the Mexuar. After being allowed through this area, bathers would then have walked down to the lower level, which was a place for undressing before bathing and relaxing afterwards; behind this can still be made out the once luxuriously appointed area where bathing equipment was kept and the more intimate ablutions performed. Taking heed of Ibn al-Khatib's warnings about contracting pneumonia through being too hasty in their progress through the *hammam*, they would then proceed as gradually as possible through a series of three vaulted rooms of increasing temperature, the last two being heated by a Roman-style *hypocaustum* (the hidden, wood-fired boiler was sold off in the 18th century to pay for restoration work in the rest of the palace). Bath attendants were always on hand with soap, combs, gloves, brushes and pails of cold water, while masseurs oiled and stretched bathers' limbs, and scraped off the dirt that oozed from their pores. The pampering continued back in the Sala de Camas, where, lying on towels arranged in the tiled alcoves, they were provided with drinks of cold water from the central fountain, herbal infusions, pastries and other small delicacies.

Anyone who has ever been to baths of this kind in present-day Morocco will know that the reality of the experience is not necessarily as sybaritic as it sounds.

'There are those who maintain that bathing produces in the body the same effects that wine does, in other words happiness and pleasure. This explains why so many people sing when they bathe.'

Ibn al-Khatib, from *The Book of Hygiene*.

Nonetheless the sight of the Alhambra's sombrely mysterious baths, with their tiles and marbled floors illuminated by dramatic shafts of light from star-shaped openings, has intensified yet further the sensual oriental reveries of many a traveller. One such person was the late 19th-century Italian author Edmondo De Amicis, who was so profoundly affected by the baths that after visiting them he began to reflect on how drably pedestrian was the modern western world when compared with the intoxicating brilliance of the Orient. 'Don't think of that,' his guide told him; 'think rather of how much that was beautiful and lovely these tubs have seen; of the little feet that played in the perfumed water, of the long hair that spread over the edges, of the great languid eyes that looked at the sky through the holes in the ceiling . . .'

The baths today, like some forbidden paradise, have been put off limits to visitors, whose route through the Nasrid Palaces has in any case been one that for centuries has led them directly from the Court of the Myrtles into what became from the Romantic period onwards the most famous and reproduced part of the whole Alhambra – the Court of the Lions.

The baths of the Alhambra underwent considerable alteration after the Christian Reconquest, including the addition of a bath (*left*) for full immersion in the water, a practice not followed by the Muslims. A narrow *tepidarium* (*right*) precedes the two hot rooms. The tiled decoration here, as throughout the baths, dates from the 19th century.

From the time that the Catholic monarchs connected the two courtyards by a passage, visitors have generally been unaware that in walking along this they are leaving the Palace of Comares and entering the Palace of the Lions, a building that was once self-contained and accessible only from the street. The stylistic differences between the two palaces are striking. In the Palace of the Lions the architecture is as complex as the ornament, and there is also a remarkable unity of conception that results partly from the building having been completed entirely within the reign of Muhammad V.

Western visitors, confused by the overall layout of the Palace of Comares, are likely at first to feel in more familiar territory on reaching the Court of the Lions. In its basic plan of a central court surrounded entirely by arcading, it owes far more to western models than to any known Islamic ones. The links between Muhammad V and the court of Peter the Cruel at Seville have encouraged some commentators to find influences from contemporary Christian architecture, notably Cistercian cloisters; but a much more obvious source of inspiration are the peristyled Roman villas described by the author Vitruvius writing in the 1st century BC.

The symmetry inherent in such traditional, classical prototypes was later stressed in the linking passageway between the two palaces, which ensured that the first glimpse of the Court of the Lions was from a point near the middle of the western side. However, the original entrance to the courtyard was from its south-western corner, which would have provided an angled and very unclassical view of the whole, and shown once again how the Alhambra's architects were concerned not so much with making people grasp the essential logic of the structure as with wooing them by lush and mysterious effects. In the case of the Court of the Lions these involved a multitude of tightly packed columns, a wealth of exotic, endlessly varied detail, and a confusion between interior and exterior as a result of having watercourses both inside and outside, and open pavilions that project into the central area. All these elements combine to create what has sometimes been called the 'Nasrid baroque' – an architecture that has upset the aesthetic sensibilities of such puritanical westerners as the Australian traveller Nina Murdoch, who, in 1935, wrote that the Court of the Lions 'seems crowded and unattractive with its hundred and twenty-four columns, its arches, its tiled pavilions, its large fountain, its eight smaller ones, and its twelve funny lions'.

The characteristically western desire to impose a rational sense of order on the apparently chaotic has manifested itself in the Court of the Lions both in the rigid route to which tourists are kept, and in the removal and paving over of the courtyard's central garden, the former luxuriance of which must once have perfectly complemented the architecture. The courtyard today without its trees, plants and flowers seems less obviously what it had originally been intended to be –

Medieval visitors to the Court of the Lions had their first glimpse of the courtyard from its south-western corner, from where this photograph is taken. The diagonal viewpoint gives the courtyard an asymmetrical character disconcerting to classical western sensibilities. The original impact would have been heightened by the abundance of exotic vegetation that was once found here.

a Persian-style enclosed garden divided into four by channels of water symbolizing the four rivers of Paradise described in the Koran. Visitors now are also prevented from inspecting at close quarters the courtyard's Fountain of the Lions, which forms the apex of the whole palace, and places at the building's heart an unresolved enigma.

The fountain, though spawning numerous life-sized reproductions throughout the world, has often caused travellers to comment on the discrepancy between its smoothly polished basin (containing sophisticated poetic evocations of water by Ibn Zamrak) and the gruff lions at its base, which even Washington Irving found so crudely carved that he ended up attributing them to 'some Christian captive'. Purely on grounds of quality rather than archaeological evidence, most writers today think of these lions as having been taken from an earlier structure, probably of the 11th century. The scholar F. P. Bargebuhr went even further and identified the lions as being from a fountain featured in an 11th-century poem full of Solomonic allusions by the Jewish author Ibn Gabirol, whom he believed was describing a palace built on this very spot by the Jewish vizier Samuel Nagralla. This in turn has fanned speculations, dating back to the Romantic era, as to whether Muhammad V's palace, like Nagralla's before it, was a conscious recreation of that most mythical of all ancient structures – the palace of King Solomon.

The existence of such esoteric symbolism is unlikely to be proved, especially as we are still not absolutely sure about either the functions of each of the different parts of the Palace of the Lions or even the purpose of the building. Was it simply another palace with its own throne room and Mexuar? Was it the home of the sultan's wives and harem or perhaps even a palace built for a favourite concubine with the name of Aisa (to whom one of the rooms is dedicated)? Or was it (as seems most probable) the Islamic equivalent of the Roman *villa urbanus* – a city villa given over principally to pleasure?

The late 14th-century Court of the Lions derives its name from the mysterious central fountain whose roughly carved and highly stylized lions (*above*) are sometimes thought to have been taken from an 11th-century palace built on this very spot. The courtyard is seen here from the centre of its western side (*right*), near the point where visitors enter Muhammad V's palace today. The symmetrical viewpoint emphasizes the underlying influence of classical villas.

'Blessed be He who gave
Muhammad a mansion, which in
beauty exceeds all other mansions;
and if not so, here is a garden
containing wonders of art,
the like of which God forbids
should elsewhere be found.
Look at this solid mass
of pearl glistening all around,
and spreading through the air its
showers of prismatic bubbles, which
fall within a circle of silvery froth,
and flow amidst other jewels,
surpassing everything in beauty,
nay exceeding the marble itself in
its whiteness and transparency . . .'

Ibn Zamrak, from the inscription
round the basin of the Fountain of the Lions,
translated by Richard Ford.

RIGHT The combination of running water and
forest-like shadows emphasizes the way in which
architecture and nature are fused so harmoniously
together in the Court of the Lions. The view here
is from the inside of one of the courtyard's
projecting pavilions.

OVERLEAF The ornamental art of Nasrid Spain
reaches its climax in the Palace of the Lions. With
its multitude of columns, its variety of capitals and
the elaborate shapes of the honeycombed arches,
hardly a single area of masonry is left undecorated.
The style that was achieved here is sometimes
known as 'Nasrid baroque'.

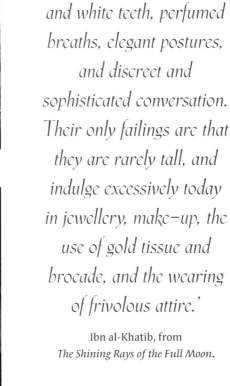

'The women are beautiful, attractively plump, graceful in physique, with loose and abundant hair, clean and white teeth, perfumed breaths, elegant postures, and discreet and sophisticated conversation. Their only failings are that they are rarely tall, and indulge excessively today in jewellery, make-up, the use of gold tissue and brocade, and the wearing of frivolous attire.'

Ibn al-Khatib, from
The Shining Rays of the Full Moon.

The higher level of the Palace of the Lions is widely thought to have been the domain of the women of the household. Two of the views reproduced here (*top* and *below left*) show what these women would have seen of the Court of the Lions from its upper southern gallery. Off this, at the heart of the presumed harem, is a tiny, secret patio (*centre left* and *right*) to which the sultan might possibly have retired after attending some of the festivities below. Though the tiling is modern, the patio is decorated with some of the rare surviving examples of mural painting in the Alhambra.

Today's circumscribed itinerary around the Court of the Lions begins in the open hall on the western side known as the Sala de Mocárabes, which is named after the *muqarnas* that hung on its ceiling until the explosion of 1590, after which they were replaced by the present baroque plasterwork. This might have been intended as a banqueting area for the sultan, who, too exhausted perhaps to return afterwards to the Palace of Comares, might have retired to the secret upper patio known today as the 'harem', which was once reached by steps from the courtyard's south-western corner.

Prevented now from climbing up to the harem, one of the Alhambra's hidden surprises, today's visitors walk down the courtyard's southern side, past the more prosaic surprise of the vast cistern hidden behind the wall to their right. This provides all the water to the Nasrid Palaces. Just beyond this a large arched opening leads into the Hall of the Abencerrages, whose central fountain is fed by one of the four channels that are arranged like a cross around the Fountain of the Lions. Those who might be regretting the loss of the *muqarnas* in the Sala de Mocárabes can find consolation here (as they will in the Hall of the Two Sisters directly opposite) in the sight of one of the Islamic world's most spectacular honeycombed ceilings, the former multicoloured appearance of which can still be imagined through extensive traces of the original polychromy. Though *muqarnas* were a form of decoration first used as early as 10th century, it was not until the creation of the Palace of the Lions that they were brought together in such extraordinary profusion, and using every known variant of the honeycomb cell.

The hall is now thought by some to have been a winter music room, where, presumably, those rapt in the sounds of song, flutes and plucked instruments could dreamily cast their eyes up to the ceiling and imagine themselves listening to the celestial music of the spheres. However, such a serene image has generally been far from the minds of later visitors to the hall, who continue to think of this as the reputed place where Muhammad IX cut off the head of the leader of the Abencerrages, and was himself later decapitated. To those many visitors who have reacted cynically to being told that the reddish-brown marks on the basin are traces of Abencerrage blood, Richard Ford responded by urging them to 'believe this and every tale of the Alhambra, a sacred spot far beyond the jurisdiction of matter-of-fact and prosaic history: do not disenchant the romance of poetry, the *genius loci* . . . above all, eschew geology; deem not these spots ferruginous, for nothing is more certain than that heroic blood never can be effaced, still less if shed in foul murder'.

RIGHT AND OVERLEAF Views of the Hall of the Abencerrages, whose central marble basin, one of the finest in the Alhambra, has oxidized iron stains popularly said to be traces of Abencerrage blood. The columned recess in the wall is thought to be where members of the household sat while watching and listening to music and dancing. The room's decorative high point is its star-shaped ceiling, with its encrustation of honeycombed forms or *muqarnas,* the colour of which was once heightened by stained-glass windows. The wall decoration was extensively restored during the 16th century.

Visitors have usually banished imaginings of Nasrid brutalities by the time they have moved on to the courtyard's eastern end, where, in the open hall known as the Hall of the Kings, Washington Irving indulged instead in visions of Catholic prelates, shaven-headed monks, knights in armour, silk-attired courtiers, Christopher Columbus and other participants at the court of Ferdinand and Isabella. This highly theatrical space, with its succession of *muqarnas*-encrusted arches creating dramatic effects of light and shade, was turned by the Catholic monarchs first into a chapel and then into a hall of justice. In earlier, more cheerful days, it probably had a festive, banqueting function comparable to that of the Sala de Mocárabes, but with the possible difference that the guests were made to sit in the three alcoves at the back.

Popular misconceptions about the total prohibition of figures in Islamic art are confounded by the presence above these alcoves of three painted panels on leather comprising the most important figurative decorations to be found in Islamic Spain. The central panel, of ten people seated in a circle, has usually been identified as a representation of the Nasrid sultans from Muhammad I to Muhammad V. The side panels, featuring a Muslim and a Christian hunting respectively a wild boar and a bear, are very much in the spirit of chivalric tapestries, if now rather obscure in their meaning. The notion of hunting and the appearance in both scenes of maidens in a tower suggest that the two men are competing for the women's favours, and that the whole might be a commentary on love. In any case, the works constitute an invaluable record of Nasrid dress in the late 14th century. Though the artist is now thought to have been a Muslim rather than a Christian, these are works clearly influenced by Italian and French art of the International Gothic period, which would have permeated to Granada by way of the court of Peter the Cruel. Further evidence of the cultural interaction between the two courts has been found in some of the hall's stuccoed decorations of naturalistic foliage. These, it is claimed, are the work of Morisco craftsmen sent by Peter the Cruel from Toledo in exchange for Granadans who worked in his palace in Seville.

BELOW AND OPPOSITE This hall, on the eastern side of the Court of the Lions, has been known variously as the Hall of the Kings or the Hall of Justice ever since it was used as a court room by the Catholic monarchs. Its wonderful theatricality, reminiscent of baroque stage design, is due to its succession of richly honey-combed forms and alternating bands of light and shade.

The Hall of the Kings is divided by its honeycombed arches into three chambers; a corner of the central one is shown here (*left*). At the back of each chamber is a recess where the sultan and his guests would have sat while attending the banquets and other festivities probably held here. The paintings on leather decorating the ceilings of the recesses (*right*) can be dated to around 1400. Although now thought to be by a Muslim artist, they are clearly the work of someone with a knowledge of Italian art of the International Gothic period. The central scene represents all the Nasrid rulers up to the time of Muhammad V (with the exception of the latter's usurpers Ismail II and Muhammad VI), while the two side ones feature romantic and chivalric scenes apparently illustrating some now forgotten legend or real-life incidents connected with the sultan kings in Christian lands.

A visit to the Palace of the Lions nears its conclusion today with the Hall of the Two Sisters, which dates back to 1362, and as such was the first part of the palace to be built. The only room in the Nasrid Palaces to have kept its original wooden doors, it is supposedly named after the two marble slabs lying in the centre of the room; however, recent evidence suggests that the walls here were once inscribed with a poem by Ibn al-Khatib that makes mention of 'Two Sisters'. This inscription, replaced by one by Ibn Zamrak after Ibn al-Khatib's disgrace in 1370, has also been used to support the thesis that the room had been intended as a new Mexuar, with the adjoining Mirador de Lindaraxa serving as another throne room. Hernando de Baeza, secretary to the Catholic monarchs and one-time interpreter to Boabdil, confused the issue yet further by saying that this room became the quarters of the sultana after the sultan had decided to return to the Palace of Comares for his official duties. Other scholars, however, remain adamant that this was just a larger, summer version of the Hall of the Abencerrages, and was given over to musical gatherings. Perhaps it is not worth allowing these irresolvable issues to interrupt our enjoyment of the honeycombed ceiling (made up of a staggering 5,000 cells) and of the stuccoed walls, which are compared in Ibn Zamrak's accompanying verse not simply to the richest of tapestries but also to the most enchanting of landscapes.

Exquisite ornamentation is also to be found in the Mirador de Lindaraxa, which has, over the arches of the window, some of the finest examples in the palace of *ataurique* interwoven with Kufic lettering. Washington Irving and other romantics seem to have been right in their belief that the Mirador was dedicated to a Moorish beauty, but her name was Aisa and not Lindaraxa, the latter word being a corruption of the Arabic phrase meaning 'the eye of Aisa's room'. The comparison of this space to an 'eye' emphasizes the room's role as a mirador, which is also stressed in an inscription around the twin-arched window that reads, 'Within this garden I am an eye beaming with happiness, and the pupil of this eye is none other than our Lord.' Originally the Mirador overlooked an orchard that stretched all the way to the Alhambra's battlements, beyond which the Albaicín would have been seen. However, this view was entirely lost when Charles V built in front of it a small courtyard surrounded by a group of apartments in which Washington Irving would later take up residence.

The courtyard, known as the Patio de Lindaraxa, was prettily landscaped in a 'Moorish style' in the late 19th century, as indeed was much of what we see between here and the Alhambra's easternmost end, where there is now a modern gate and bridge leading to the gardens of the Generalife. Making your way today from the Palace of the Lions towards the eastern gate, you can easily forget that the 'Moorish' gardens around you were laid out in recent times over what had been a maze of alleys and buildings that still await full excavation.

The Hall of the Two Sisters is dominated by what the poet Ibn Zamrak described as its 'celestial vault'. This extraordinary honeycombed ceiling, comprising 5,000 cells, is the most intricate one not only in the Alhambra but also in the whole of the Islamic world. All the known variations of the honeycomb form were used in its construction.

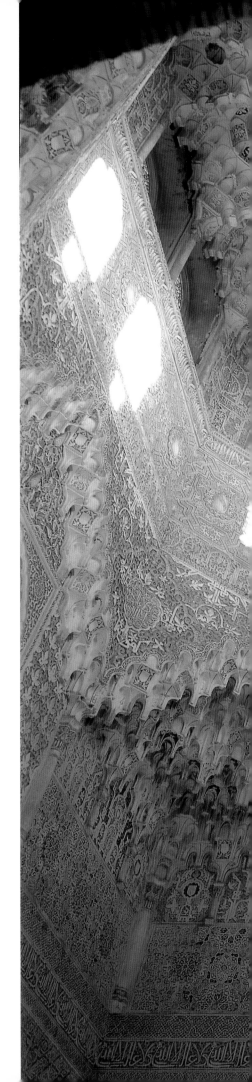

'How much pleasure for the eyes is here!' runs one of the many celebrated lines by Ibn Zamrak covering the walls of the Hall of the Two Sisters. The room is seen here (*below*) with the Mirador of Lindaraxa in the background. A fragment of Ibn Zamrak's verse is featured in this detail from one of its wall decorations (*right*).

OVERLEAF The Mirador of Lindaraxa (*left*), which once had views of open countryside, looks out today over the Patio de Lindaraxa (*right*), a 16th-century creation landscaped during the Romantic era. The marble fountain was placed in the Patio in 1626 (the basin was taken from outside the Mexuar).

'You have dressed the palace walls in a fabric unmatched even by the cloths of Yemen ...'

Ibn Zamrak, inscription from the Hall of the Two Sisters.

THIS PAGE AND OPPOSITE
The addition by Charles V
of residential quarters on
the northern side of the
Palace of the Lions led to
the creation of two patios
of charming simplicity.
This was the part of
the Alhambra where
Washington Irving lodged.

A 16th-century gallery (*above*) connects the Tower of Comares with the originally free-standing Peinador de la Reina. The view east from the Peinador is towards the tower of the early 14th-century Palace of the Partal, which is seen here (*opposite*) rising above a group of houses built by Muhammad V; the Partal's distinctive palm trees, the only ones in the Alhambra, loom in the background. This same viewpoint was adopted by the 19th-century British artist John Frederick Lewis in a much reproduced watercolour in the British Museum.

Three main streets once served this royal city, including a central one – directly below the southern walls of the Nasrid Palaces – that went in between the Palace of the Lions and a domed structure containing the royal cemetery or *rauda*. Corresponding closely to the Alhambra's present main thoroughfare was a southern street that linked the Alcazaba with the eastern and principal end of the medina, passing on the way the Alhambra's main mosque, of which only the adjoining baths remain, the rest having been pulled down in favour of the uninspiring late baroque church of Santa María la Blanca. The third and probably most important street ran underneath the northern battlements, and has some evocative surviving stretches, discreetly tucked away between walls of brick, rubble and stucco.

Of the Alhambra's other palaces, the main one still standing is that of the Partal, which seems today like a porticoed garden pavilion, missing as it does the three other structures that enclosed its now exposed pool. South-east of here are the foundations of the 15th-century palace known as that of the Court of Tendilla, which was the official residence of the governors of the Alhambra until 1717, when the post was abolished and the building pulled down. The Palace of the Abencerrages, dating back to the 13th century, was destroyed by the French when they blew up the Gate of the Seven Floors, and was further devastated as recently as 1957, when its buried remains were partially appropriated for the building of a car park. Fragments of a *villa urbanus*, built by Muhammad III in the early 14th century and later remodelled by Muhammad V, are visible in the Monastery of San Francisco, which was once the temporary resting place of the bodies of the Catholic monarchs, and is now a state-run hotel or *parador*.

Though most of the former royal city no longer exists, and needs a considerable imagination to reconstruct, there are always surprises for those who are patient. Behind the formidable walls of the northern defensive towers, for instance, are fabulous interiors that are like palaces in their own right – a feature apparently unique to the Alhambra and one that further illustrates the way in which Islamic Granada is like a Russian doll of worlds within worlds.

Among these structures is the elegant early 14th-century lantern tower known as the Peinador de la Reina, which was joined by Charles V to the Patio de Lindaraxa and painted inside with Italianate figure scenes and arabesques while being prepared as a boudoir for his wife, the Empress Isabel: in one of its surviving Arabic inscriptions Yusuf I appears to have substituted his own name for that of his deposed and disgraced grandfather, Abul-Juyush Nasr, thus unwittingly giving *carte blanche* to all those 18th- and 19th-century travellers who would deface the walls with their own signatures.

The tower of the early 14th-century Palace of the Partal (*left*), encased within an area landscaped in modern times (*above* and *below right*), can easily be mistaken today for a garden pavilion. It is the sole surviving part of a four-winged structure that originally stood around the present pool, the Alhambra's largest expanse of water. The pool's two crouching lions (*centre right*), which were taken in the 19th century from the Maristan hospital in the Albaicín, have now been placed in the safer but less picturesque surroundings of the Alhambra Museum.

Similarly curious features are to be seen inside the late 14th-century Torre de los Picos, which has traces of painted geometrical motifs and quadripartite vaulting suggestive of Christian influence if not actual workmanship. Christian slaves were certainly active in the nearby Torre de la Cautiva, a structure built during the reign of Yusuf I and embellished thoughout its interior with a glorious coating of stucco ornamentation featuring inscriptions by the only known Alhambra poet not to have met a violent end, Ibn al-Yayyab, the mentor of Ibn al-Khatib.

Finally, at the furthest end of the Alhambra's grounds, comes the Torre de las Infantas, which has stucco decorations that have been dated to the 15th century on the grounds of diminished ornamental inventiveness. No trace of decline, however, was noticed by Washington Irving, who thought that the tower though 'not generally shown to strangers, is well worthy of attention, for the interior is equal, for beauty of architecture and delicacy of ornament, to any part of the palace'. As with other romantics he was attracted by the tower's remote and wooded situation, and by the tale that it had once housed the sultan's daughters. He was told this by the 'young and buxom Andalucían damsel' who lived there during his day and first appeared to him with her head covered in flowers, staring from the tower's upper window.

The Alhambra's northern walls, seen here from the entrance to the Generalife, are marked by a series of towers that are like palaces in their own right. Towering above them to the left is the Alhambra's former mosque, now the church of Santa Maria la Blanca.

*'This bastion before you,
clothed in gold like a king,
is a sturdy defence
against our enemies that
shields within a brightly
shining palace . . .'*

Ibn al-Yayyab, from an inscription
on the walls of the Torre de la Cautiva.

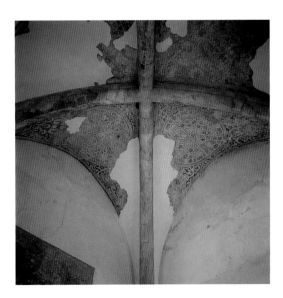

LEFT The Torre de los Picos, a late
13th- or early 14th-century structure
named after the pointed forms of
its battlements, has many of the
characteristics of a Christian Gothic
structure, such as the slit windows in the
cellar (*above left*), and the quadripartite
vaulting on the main floor (*centre left*),
which is notable for its traces of painted
geometrical decoration. The architect
is likely to have been a Christian, and
possibly a slave. A glimpse of the
northern battlements can be seen from
one of its paired windows (*below left*).

RIGHT The Torre de las Infantas, which
is sometimes said to be one of the last
Nasrid additions to the Alhambra, is
romantically believed to be the place
where the sultan's daughters lived.

OVERLEAF The Torre de la Cautiva derives
its name from the popular legend that
this was where the Sultan Abul-Hasan
kept his beloved mistress, Isabel de Solís,
the Christian captive for whom he
abandoned his wife Aisa. The most
splendidly decorated of all the
Alhambra's towers, it was built during
the reign of Yusuf I, and is extensively
inscribed with lines by Ibn al-Yayyab.

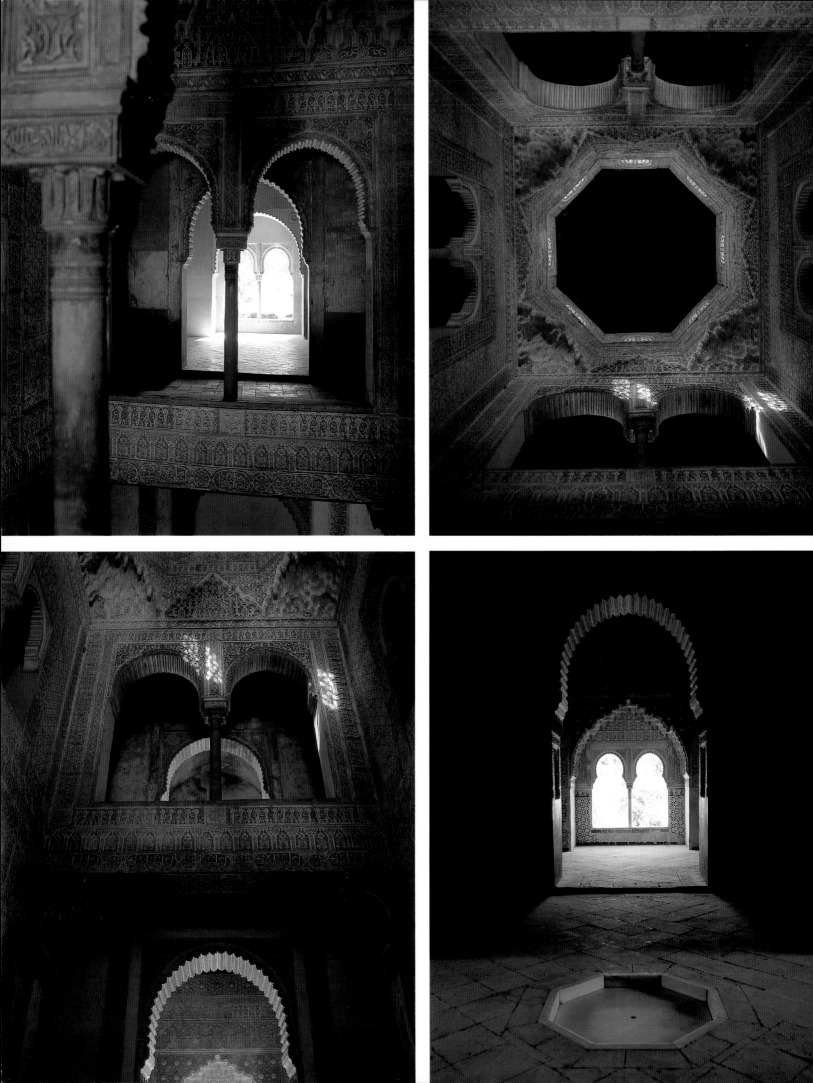

Those who have followed the Alhambra's northern walls all the way to the Torre de las Infantas will emerge soon afterwards at the gate built in 1971 to link the royal city with the former Nasrid property of the Generalife, the most important of Granada's outlying Islamic villas. Separated from the Alhambra by a leafy ravine planted on its lower slopes with orchards and vegetable gardens, the Generalife was once reached from the Alhambra by a path halfway up the Cuesta de los Chinos. The approach alone was enough for early travellers to feel that they were nearing Paradise, such was the abundance of the vegetation and the overwhelming perfume of aromatic plants. An ecstatic Gautier, who likened the surroundings to how he imagined 'a virgin forest in America', described an overgrown path climbing up through fig trees with 'enormous shining leaves', oaks, pistachio trees, laurels, aloes and a wilderness of flowers streaked with

The northern battlements of the Alhambra look out across a cultivated valley towards the summer palace of the Generalife (*above*), from where they can be seen, with the Torres de las Infantas and de la Cautiva, rising picturesquely above an ocean of green (*right*). The orchards and the fields between the two hills were laid out by the Moors and probably give a good idea of how the Generalife's gardens were originally planted.

the scarlet blooms of pomegranates and the white petals of jasmine.

The Generalife itself, whose name has been interpreted as 'the noblest of villas', has inspired passions going back almost to the time of its foundation in 1319 – the date that appears on one of the white-washed walls of its pavilions. Ibn al-Khatib referred to the charm of its running waters, to its sweet air and to its surrounding covering of trees so thick that the light could barely penetrate through the leaves; others spoke of its abundant roses and gentle breeze. Ibn Zamrak concluded that the place was 'the throne of Granada' – an opinion apparently shared by the first known Christian visitors, Hieronymus Münzer and Andrea Navagiero, who devoted more pages to this 'most excellent of gardens' than to the whole of the Alhambra.

The Generalife, though fortunate in the wealth of early accounts relating to it, has fared less well than the Nasrid Palaces in terms of preservation. The delicate summer pavilions, after suffering from repeated restorations and remodellings during four centuries, had to be extensively rebuilt after a disastrous fire in 1959. Meanwhile the dense wood that encased them was tamed first in the 1930s with the laying-out of the long terrace of gardens that led up to the villa, and then in 1951 with the creation of an open-air theatre for the International Festival of Music and Dance.

The box hedges, cypresses, pools, fountains and sea of flowers that purport to reproduce the Islamic gardens of old probably correspond more to romantic notions of what 'Moorish gardens' should be like than to historical reality. Few achievements of a civilization are as ephemeral as gardens; and recent and continuing research into the Islamic ones of the Generalife indicates that much of what we see today was probably originally a working garden, with orchards, vegetables, vines and even livestock.

Yet for all the changes that have occurred in the Generalife, and for all the crowds of tourists that now generally make the tranquil enjoyment of the place impossible, the gardens have retained most of the elements that make up the ideal garden outlined by the 14th-century Granadan author and agricultural theorist Ibn Luyun – a south-facing position, terraces of different heights, a central open pavilion for the afternoon siesta, myrtles and climbing roses, paths shaded by pergolas, a long pool flanked by potted plants, a hidden pool fully protected by trees and an overall layout longer than it is wide so that 'the eye shall not tire on contemplating it'.

Islamic visitors to the Generalife would have dismounted at the lower courtyard and climbed from there up to the endlessly photographed Patio de la Acequia, with its elongated flower-lined watercourses providing a delightful approach to the main pavilion. The jets of water that so enchant today's visitors are late 19th-century additions; but the overall design, with its central short arms of water that divide the long courtyard into four, was restored to its presumed original state on the basis of archaeological evidence uncovered after the 1959 fire. The courtyard might well have had a considerable influence on the architects of the Alhambra: the disposition of structures around its edge prefigured the design of the Court of the Myrtles, while its arrangement as a 'paradise garden' was later perfected in the Court of the Lions.

Steps lead from the main pavilion up to the more discreetly situated Court of the Queen's Cypress, which is centred on a dark shaded pond and was entirely remodelled in Renaissance times. At the very top of the gardens visitors would once have reached a small mosque or oratory, which peered above the surrounding trees, and enjoyed wonderful, extensive views towards the Alhambra. Though this mosque was replaced by the present late 19th-century mirador, the stepped path climbing up to it is still flanked, as in Islamic times, with white-washed walls that have channels scooped out of them which allow water to run down in winding torrents. This last feature seems to have been of especial fascination to Andrea Navagiero, who loved the way in which the water level could be raised so that the fast-flowing streams would suddenly and dramatically overflow the walls and soak unsuspecting passers-by, much to the hilarity of onlookers.

By the time most of today's visitors reach this staircase, the sun has already begun to set and closing bells are ringing. A tour of the Alhambra and the Generalife has come to an end, but, as the light fades and the crowds disperse, another Alhambra begins to reveal itself. Harsh daylight, according to Richard Ford, merely exposes the monument's ravages and faults, 'dispels the dreamy, haunted air' and makes us 'examine, measure and criticize'. At twilight, however, the Alhambra 'becomes entirely a vision of the past', and 'all is given up again to the past and the Moor'. Only when the moon rises does the Alhambra manage finally to release itself from the shackles of reality, and emerge as the timeless, indestructible palace defined by romantics as 'the fabric of the Genii'.

Neatly arranged gardens laid out in the 20th century (*opposite*) precede the original villa of the Generalife, which has as its centrepiece the much restored Patio de la Acequia. The patched-up wall (*above*) is an indication of this courtyard's former ruinous state.

OVERLEAF A neo-Gothic mirador (*above left*), built in the 19th century on the site of an Islamic oratory, crowns the highest part of the Generalife. One of the two flights of steps leading up to it is modern (*right*), but the other (*below left*) dates back to Moorish times and was greatly admired by the Venetian 16th-century traveller Andrea Navagiero for its wonderful, water-supporting balustrades.

> *'An open pavilion, intended for the hours of rest, should rise up in the centre, surrounded by climbing roses, myrtles and other such pleasing garden plants . . .'*

Ibn Luyun, from his description
of an ideal garden in his
Treatise on Agriculture.

The gleaming white mass of the Generalife, floating high on a green sea of vegetation (*above left*), was altered to an even greater extent than the Alhambra itself by changes and restoration. The character of the Patio de la Acequia was effected by the enlargement in the 16th century of the northern pavilion (*centre left* and *below left*), and by the placing in the Romantic era of the famous jets of water. The patio's southern pavilion (*right*) was originally the more important of the two.

THE FABRIC
OF THE GENII

Visions of the Alhambra

From impressions and sketches derived from his visit to Granada in 1833, the British artist David Roberts produced numerous fantastical views of the Alhambra, such as this oil painting *View of the Alhambra* (*left*) commissioned in 1837 by the Marquis of Lansdowne. The largest known oil in Roberts' career, it was inspired by the celebrated view of the Alhambra from the top of the Albaicín (*above*). As well as greatly distorting the Alcazaba, Roberts pandered to exotic British notions of Spain by transforming the foreground into a scene of picturesquely costumed figures dancing in front of Castilian-looking buildings shaded by giant palms (trees uncharacteristic of Granada).

155

THE IMAGE OF THE ALHAMBRA as an enchanted palace was not merely the creation of romantic travellers drunk on moonlight, ruins and Moorish fantasies. It was also an image dating back to the twilight of Nasrid Granada, when the struggle between Moors and Christians took on a gloss of glamour and poetry, and turned the eyes of Europe to a remote and mountainous land of increasingly mythical reputation. The writer Garci Rodríguez de Montalvo could even claim in 1508 that the 'chivalric deeds' of the Reconquest of Granada inspired his definitive version of one of Spain's earliest and most influential romances of chivalry, *Amadís de Gaula*, an epic filled with giants, magicians and dragons.

The Moorish mythology that would so passionately enthuse travellers of the Romantic era came into being with the collapse of Moorish Granada, and found its tales not in the Golden Age of Granada but rather in such aspects of recent history as the beheading of the Abencerrages in the Palace of the Lions, Abul-Hasan's love for the Christian captive whom he renamed Zoraya, and Boabdil's last sigh on leaving Granada ('Weep like a woman,' his mother famously told him, 'you who have not defended your kingdom like a man').

Tales such as these, so fresh in the minds of the Christian conquerors, would have been avidly absorbed by travellers who needed to hear stories that lived up to the high-flown imaginings provoked by the sight of the Alhambra and other exotic marvels. The poetic distortions of history that were already widely circulating in the immediate wake of the Reconquest pandered to Christian notions of Moorish savagery, and, above all, of Moorish sensuality. One of the first known Christian visitors, Hieronymus Münzer, visiting the Alhambra in 1494, was teased and titillated with numerous anecdotes supplied by its first governor, the Count of Tendilla. Among these was the unlikely story of how Granada's sultans spied on the women of the harem as they entered the palace baths naked; the one who caught the sultan's fancy was then thrown an orange as a signal that she 'should lie with him that night'.

Amorous tales of Granada's last Moors proved endlessly popular, especially if these entailed illicit and impossible affairs between members of rival Moorish factions, or, better still, between Moors and Christians. Affairs of this kind, celebrated in numerous 15th-century frontier ballads, gave rise to a remarkably successful anonymous novel of *c.*1550 entitled *The Story of the Abencerrage and the Beautiful Jarifa*, which related the supposedly true story of the love between a noble Moorish captive and the daughter of the Christian governor of the Andalucían town of Coín. In turn it greatly influenced what would become the most important source for romantic visions of Moorish history – Ginés Pérez de Hita's two-volume historical novel commonly known as *The Civil Wars of Granada* (1593). This remarkable blend of fact, fiction and frontier ballads features a lengthy account of the second Morisco uprising of 1569–71, in which the author himself took part. But it is famous principally for its stories of the Abencerrages and their rivals the Zegris, notably the secret romance of the Abencerrage leader Aben-Hamet and Boabdil's betrothed, 'Zoraida', who had daily trysts with her lover behind a rose-bush in the Generalife.

Zoraida, Zoraya and other such variants on this name as Zaida, Zoraima, Zelima, Zobeida, Zulima, Zuléma and Zulnar, came to pepper the many Moorish-inspired

novels, poems, plays, ballets and operas that began to proliferate after 1600. In England the poet John Dryden helped greatly to popularize this mythical late 15th-century Granada with his once famous tragedy *The Conquest of Granada* (1672), which had Nell Gwyn starring in the love affair between Zoraida and Aben-Hamet (whose names he changed respectively to Almanzor and Almahide). In France meanwhile, the intrigues of the Granadan court were promoted at first in staged musical works, such as Pancrace Royer's 'historical ballet' of 1739, *Zaïda, Queen of Granada*, which was later the subject of an opera by the seventeen-year-old Mozart.

All these Moorish fantasies helped to make the names of the Alhambra and the Generalife celebrated throughout Europe in the 17th and 18th centuries. Yet they did not encourage large numbers of people to go to Granada during this period, which, as late as 1792, was described by a French prisoner in the town as being more 'famous' than it was 'known'. Though sightseers had begun coming here in significant numbers from at least the middle years of the 18th century, these early visitors were motivated less by a taste in Moorish romance than by intellectual curiosity and a desire to record scientifically, typical of this age of the dilettante.

The Spaniards themselves, despite having civic authorities and a new royal family that were neglectful of the Alhambra, were deeply conscious of the monument's enormous importance not just as a repository of myth but as a supreme architectural achievement worthy of preservation and study. Indeed, one of the first acts of Spain's newly formed academy of fine arts, the Academia de San Fernando, was to commission in 1756 a record of the Alhambra's decorations and architecture with a view to eventual restoration. Emotional and artistic prejudices were not allowed to compromise the objectivity of this project, which was carried out with laborious care over four decades, and with the participation of the future neo-classical architect of the Prado Museum, Juan de Villanueva.

While Villanueva and others were slowly preparing the eventual two volumes of *Las antiguedades árabes de España* (1780, 1804), an especially large number of English visitors had begun making their way to the Alhambra. Their incentives were a love of intrepid travel and an intellectual interest in a monument that would do much to promote the growth in England of the Gothic revival.

One of the earliest of these visitors was the politician William Pitt's eccentric nephew James. His unpublished notes of a journey through Spain in 1760 are fascinating as the spontaneous jottings of a man trying to come to terms with an architecture that must have seemed particularly exotic to a generation unaccustomed to descriptions and reproductions of it. In refreshing contrast to the effusive outpourings of later, full-blown romantics, Pitt's commentary was a measured one.

The Alhambra became a legend in Europe long before many people had any idea of what it actually looked like. Johann Heinrich Müntz's 1750 design for a pavilion in London's Kew Gardens, for instance, though known as the 'Alhambra', bore no relation whatsoever to its namesake.

ABOVE Richard Twiss included in his *Travels through Portugal and Spain* (1775) one of the first relatively realistic views of the Alhambra to be featured in an English publication. The accuracy of this work is due to the engraver having illegally plundered an illustration scheduled to appear in a scholarly study undertaken by Spain's Academia de San Fernando.

OPPOSITE The sober and scholarly-looking title page of James Murphy's *Arabian Antiquities of Spain* (1813–15) is belied by such pictorial distortions of the Alhambra as a cathedral-like view of the Hall of the Abencerrages.

He even managed the rarely-to-be-repeated feat of finding fault in the Generalife, which he described as 'small and ill-laid out, the water being thrown up in little fountains, and the trees spoilt with trellace'. However, his primary interest in studying all these Moorish remains was to ponder an issue of vital importance to the burgeoning English Romantic movement – the development of the Gothic style, and the extent to which this might have been influenced by the Moorish or 'Saracenic' style.

Defeated in the end by the strangeness of the architecture, Pitt was unable to reach any definite conclusion. 'Tho' I doubt not ... that the Moorish is entirely a peculiar style and brought with them out of Africa, I cannot so well determine to my satisfaction whether it is, like the old Gothic, a corruption from the Roman ... or brought with them out of Arabia.' Later English travellers had few such hesitations. The Alhambra became in their descriptions the ultimate example of a style so important for the evolution of Gothic architecture that even the tracery of Gothic stained-glass windows was thought by some to derive from filigree Moorish stuccowork.

More than just a sourcebook for specific Gothic forms, the Alhambra came to be viewed as an illustration of the irrational, anti-classical qualities advocated by two of 18th-century England's leading aesthetic theorists, Edmund Burke and William Gilpin. The publication in 1757 of Burke's views *On the Sublime and Beautiful* gave an intellectual dignity to the feelings of incomprehension and indefinable emotion experienced by Pitt and others in front of the Alhambra. 'It is our ignorance of things,' Burke wrote, 'that causes all our admiration and chiefly excites our passions.' But the confusion within the minds of the Alhambra's admirers was so great that the monument came to be seen in terms both of the Sublime (the vital ingredient of which was the ability to inspire terror) and of its antithesis the Beautiful, which was suggestive of serenity, small scale and delicate detailing. From the 1780s onwards the debate as to whether the Alhambra was more Sublime than Beautiful or vice versa was further complicated by the addition of Gilpin's term Picturesque, which was certainly the most appropriate of the three words to convey the Alhambra's asymmetries and irregularities, not to mention its ever more ruinous condition.

In 1760 Pitt had thought the Alhambra 'so ill-kept that it will probably not last many generations longer'. Nearly thirty years later, the French traveller Jean-François Peyron found the marble floors within the palaces to be 'half-broken and over-grown with weeds and moss', and was dismayed to see such a beautiful work of art as the Fountain of the Lions 'abandoned, so to speak, in the middle of rubbish'. The palaces, after having served for a while as a military hospital, were further damaged in 1798 by being partly appropriated as the official residence of the governor of Granada, who was said to have used much of the woodwork for fires and allowed farm animals to run around the halls. The indignation of travellers at the sight of all this decay and neglect often hid an unconfessed delight in the poignant and picturesque effects resulting from such combinations as donkeys, colourfully dressed gypsy women and grand, crumbling walls. An underlying relish of pathos and nostalgia can be detected even in the deep concern shown for the Alhambra in 1810 by the English traveller William Jacob. 'Without repair, to which the finances are inadequate,' he predicted,' it will in a few years be a pile of ruins; its voluptuous apartments, its stately columns, and its lofty walls, will be mingled together, and no memorial be left in Spain of a people who once governed the peninsula.'

Under the delayed influence perhaps of Burke, the spirit of scientific enquiry that had characterized visitors to the Alhambra of Pitt's generation gave way by the early 19th century to ever more emotional and unscientific responses to the monument. Careful stylistic analysis and thoughtful reflections on architecture had been succeeded by the blatant expression of feelings and prejudices fuelled – in the case of Protestant travellers – by an unflinching belief in the supremacy of Moorish civilization over Spanish Catholicism. Though obsessed by the Sublime they failed to find this quality in the massive and awe-inspiring Palace of Charles V, which they generally regarded as no less of a disgrace to Spain than the fanatical Cardinal Cisneros. Instead, in their search for the Sublime, they began to perceive the Nasrid Palaces in a totally distorted way, as can be seen in the engravings of the English architect James Cavanagh Murphy.

Murphy, who came to Andalucía in 1802, spent seven years there engaged in the posthumously published *Arabian Antiquities of Spain* (1813–15), which was the first work in English to rival the Academy's *Las antiguedades árabes de España*. The striking differences between the two publications are indicative of the clash between the ideals of the Enlightenment and those of the early Romantic period. The editors of the Spanish volumes prided themselves on their scrupulous accuracy, and even criticized foreigners for being 'unreliable, inaccurate and generally arbitrary' in their transcriptions of the texts on the Alhambra's walls. Murphy, in contrast, was so concerned with emphasizing the Sublime aspects of the Alhambra that he gave rooms such as the Hall of the Abencerrages the towering proportions of Gothic cathedrals, and, more ridiculously still, transformed the intimate Court of the Lions into an echoing, intimidating space grander even than the Great Mosque at Córdoba.

Now that the concerns of science were being overwhelmed by the demands of the imagination, the myths of Nasrid Spain acquired an importance greater than ever before, and became for the first time the principal reason for visits to Granada.

This renewed fascination with the Moorish past was part of the growing western obsession with the Orient – an obsession that had developed at a time when the threat of Islam to the West had largely receded, and Europeans had begun increasingly to harbour colonial designs on North Africa and the Near East. It was by no means coincidental that the two countries with the greatest colonial ambitions in these areas, Britain and France, should have given birth to most of the leading European artists and writers associated with Orientalism, and that nearly everyone who succumbed to this mania should have ended up visiting Granada – a place that came to be known from the early 19th century as the 'gateway to the Orient'.

The improvement in communications and standards of accommodation in Spain encouraged increasing numbers of travellers to head south to Andalucía. There they hoped to experience all the thrills of the Orient without having to put up with the genuine dangers, difficulties and discomforts that they would have faced in the Orient itself. British travellers now came to be equalled in numbers by the French, one of the most influential of whom was the writer François René de Chateaubriand, who visited the Alhambra in 1807 and found it 'worthy to be ranked even with the temples of Greece'. This comment, so indicative of the changing canons of western taste, was followed by his similarly revealing observation that the monument was 'one of those buildings from the Thousand and One Nights, that one sees less in reality than in dreams'. 'It is,' he further enthused to a friend, 'pure enchantment, magic, glory, love; it is like nothing one has ever known.'

Three years after Chateaubriand's visit, Granada was occupied by French troops, who took up residence in the Alhambra. Demonstrating what Washington Irving would later call 'that enlightened taste which has ever distinguished the French nation in their conquests', they set about rescuing the monument 'from the absolute ruin and desolation that were overwhelming it'. They repaired the roofs, protected the halls and galleries from the weather, cultivated the gardens, renewed the watercourses, and made the fountains work again. But, on being forced to leave the Alhambra in 1812, they blew up eight of its Moorish towers, thus effectively destroying once and for all the monument's military importance, and giving the place a more abandoned air than ever. By the 1820s the governor of Granada had moved back to the lower town, and the garrison was reduced to a handful of invalid soldiers, whose main duty was to guard the remaining towers, some of which served occasionally as prisons. Water no longer flowed into the fountains, and the garden that the French had replanted in the Court of the Lions was growing into a flowery jungle of sunflowers, larkspur and marigolds. This was the state in which the Alhambra would be seen by a new generation of romantic travellers who streamed into Spain as a result of all the international publicity generated first by the Peninsular War and then by the appearance in 1827 of Chateaubriand's novel, *The Last of the Abencerrages*.

The writer Richard Ford used one of his many amateur sketches of the Alhambra as the basis of this ambitious gouache depicting the towers blown up by the French in 1812.

This extraordinarily popular work shamelessly took its inspiration from a mixture of *The Story of the Abencerrage and the Beautiful Jarifa* and Pérez de Hita's account of the ill-fated relationship between Aben-Hamet and Zoraida. Updating the action to the aftermath of the Christian Reconquest of 1492, the book opens among the exiled Moors in Tunis, who are described as living in a state of permanent nostalgia for 'the Paradise of Granada': 'mothers repeated its name even to babies at the breast, lulling them to sleep with Zegri and Abencerrage ballads'. Eventually, the book's young hero can no longer contain his curiosity, and crosses over to Spain to see for himself the land of his forefathers. After discovering the very rose bush in the Generalife where his father seduced the beautiful Alfaima, he promptly encounters by chance the lovely daughter of a Christian nobleman, and is taken by her on a twilight tour of the Alhambra.

Chateaubriand himself had not been back to the monument since 1807, and the description included in the novel has all the characteristic exaggerations and imprecisions of a place remembered from the distant past. 'He believed himself transported to the entrance of some palace, such as one finds described in the Arabian tales. Long galleries, canals of white marble, bordered by flowering lemon and orange trees, fountains, lonely courts, everywhere met his eye; and, through long porticoed

arches, he perceived other labyrinths, new enchantments.' After such an ecstatic experience in the Alhambra, the Abencerrage can only fall hopelessly in love with the young Christian woman, who reciprocates his emotions no less passionately, evidently finding in him a noble savage as worthy of his lineage as Fenimore Cooper's 'last of the Mohicans' (Cooper's novel of that name appeared the year before Chateaubriand's). Their love is of course doomed, and the last of the noble Abencerrages ends up dying alone many years later in Tunis, where he is buried in a now neglected and unremarkable tomb visited only by birds.

Orientalist fervour was stirred up into a frenzy by this Abencerrage romance. It reached feverish new peaks two years later with the publication of *Les Orientales*, an epic poem by Victor Hugo, a writer whose early literary ambitions had been fired by an adulation of the works of Chateaubriand. By the time of *Les Orientales*, Hugo's worship of Chateaubriand had been tempered by contact with the man himself, who turned out to be cold and reserved. Nonetheless the impact of the latter's steamy and evocative novel was sufficient for Hugo to include in his poem what would become some of the most quoted lines ever written on the Alhambra:

> The Alhambra! The Alhambra! Palace that the Genies
> Have gilded like a dream filled with harmonies,
> Fortress of festooned and crumbling battlements
> Where at night magic syllables resound
> When the moon, shining through a thousand Arab arches
> Spangles the walls with white clover!

Hugo had never been to Granada, and was never to go; but his poem significantly contributed to the transformation of this sleepy place into what French romantics such as the Marquis de Custine were soon terming the 'capital of the world'.

A date of key importance in the romantic history of Granada was the year 1829, for it saw the arrival, in April, of the young Washington Irving, an American diplomat then engaged in research for a book on *The Conquest of Granada*. Along with his aristocratic Russian colleague, Prince Dolgouriki, Irving was 'royally quartered' in the apartments of the Palace of Comares formerly occupied by the Governor of Granada, and maintained by a peasant woman known as Tía Antonia. 'Here then,' Irving wrote to a friend, 'I am nestled in one of the most remarkable, romantic and delicious spots in the world. I breakfast in the Saloon of the Ambassadors, among the flowers and fountains in the Court of the Lions, and when I am not occupied with my pen I lounge with my book about these oriental apartments, or stroll about the courts, and gardens, and arcades, by day or night, with no-one to interrupt me. It absolutely appears to me like a dream, or as if I am spell-bound in some fairy palace.'

Prince Dolgouriki soon had to leave, though not before presenting to the governor a visitors' book intended to prevent the likes of Chateaubriand from writing their names on the Alhambra's walls. But Irving was determined to stay on, and caused much inconvenience and consternation through his decision to do so in some deserted and dangerously decayed rooms above the small courtyard built by Charles V in the Palace of the Lions. He remained there until 29 July, when, 'after having passed between two or three months in a kind of oriental dream', he was posted to London.

The outcome of Irving's dream was his book *The Alhambra* (1832), which, under the later title of *Tales of the Alhambra*, is still sold in Granada today in a cheap edition in a score of languages. Though purporting to be an account of his stay in the Alhambra, interwoven with tales from history and legend, it was rightly included, together with Chateaubriand's *Last of the Abencerrages*, in the 1835 volume of the series 'Standard Novels'. The epigraph of this series was the phrase: 'No kind of literature is so generally attractive as fiction.' Repetitive, uncritically enthusiastic and in need of a good editor, the work established a semi-fictional genre of writing about the Alhambra that has been perpetuated to the present day. Central to this genre is the authors' insistence on the uniqueness of their experiences. In the case of Irving and fellow early travellers this meant having stayed within the Nasrid Palaces, and suggesting, falsely, that there was no one else around to disturb their reveries other than the odd picturesque local or suitably fantastical visitor (preferably a Muslim with turbanned head, or some beautiful female). Irving, to his credit, was at least able to provide one of the most famous explanations as to why the Alhambra has so often deprived its admirers of their rational critical faculties: 'The peculiar charm of this old dreamy palace is its power of calling up vague reveries and picturings of the past, and thus clothing naked realities with the illusions of the memory and the imagination.'

Washington Irving at about the time when he wrote *The Alhambra* (1832).

Irving's stay in 1829 initiated the most intense decade in the romantic history of the Alhambra. Two years after him came Richard Ford, who was also offered the use of the apartments looked after by Tía Antonia. However, as he was with his family and servants, he was slightly alarmed by the prospect of staying in rooms that were said to be more picturesque than comfortable. In a letter to a British diplomat in Madrid, he confessed that 'as my children and English servants have no taste for the Moorish picturesque, but a great notion of the more humble gratifications proceeding from a comfortable home and well-appointed kitchen, I am rather inclined to put up with the unromantic reality of some good ready-furnished house'. In the end he was able to overcome these worries after ensuring that the rooms had been thoroughly overhauled beforehand by a group of decorators and carpenters. The visit turned out to be a great success, and Ford and his family returned to the Alhambra two summers later to be put up this time in quarters modernized to his satisfaction in the Palace of the Partal.

Ford shared Irving's élitist belief that the only way to understand the Alhambra was to stay there; but in other respects he was very different from Irving. For a start he had a great sense of the ridiculous. His writings on the Alhambra, contained in his still indispensable *Handbook to Spain* of 1845, have perhaps never been bettered as a general introduction to the monument, combining as they do an engaging mix of scholarship, lyricism and earthy humour. Though beautifully conveying all the timeless magnificence of the architecture (especially at night, when the moon's 'wan rays tip the filigree arches, and give a depth to the shadows, and a misty undefined magnitude to the saloons beyond'), Ford was always aware of the mortal failings of the structure, of the often absurd background presence of the modern world, and of the possibility that the Alhambra might 'disappoint those who, fonder of the present and a cigar than of the past and the abstract, arrive heated with the hill, and

Richard Ford, seen below in three watercolours by Joaquin Bequier, dressed in the picturesque costume of a Spanish *majo* or low-class dandy. Ford executed numerous Spanish sketches that later helped him while compiling his celebrated *Handbook to Spain* (1845). His drawing of the Tower of Comares (*opposite above*) reveals him as a less meticulous draughtsman than his talented and beautiful wife Harriet, who is represented here by her sketch of the Court of the Lions (*opposite below*).

are thinking of getting back to an ice, a dinner, and a siesta'. Indeed, it was through Ford's uncommon ability simultaneously to mock and to enthuse that he succeeded more than any of his contemporaries in giving his descriptions of the Alhambra a sense of a real place.

The third and perhaps most visually aware of the celebrated literary visitors to the Alhambra of this generation was Théophile Gautier, who had in fact studied to be a painter before taking up writing under the overwhelming impact of Hugo's *Les Orientales*. Sporting thereafter an Egyptian costume through the streets of Paris, he dreamt for many years of the Orient, but had to content himself at first with Spain, whither he finally set off in the late spring of 1840. Depressed and bored by Madrid, a place so drab and modern in comparison with the oriental towns of his imagination, he became positively manic with joy on reaching the infinitely more provincial Granada. Here he would spend over a quarter of his eventual five-month stay in Spain. The days of being offered apartments within the Alhambra were now long gone, but the local authorities were apparently still sufficiently lax as to allow Gautier and his companion to camp out for a few nights around the Court of the Lions. Alternating their base camp between the Hall of the Abencerrages and that of the Two Sisters, Gautier and his friend made themselves comfortable with the aid of mattresses, a copper lamp, an earthenware jug and several bottles of sherry wine, which they kept cool in the by now restored fountain in the centre of the courtyard. Whether true or not, Gautier's proud boast to have slept rough in the Nasrid Palaces (no other traveller is known to have done so) would enter the mythology of the Alhambra following the publication in 1842 of his *Journey to Spain*.

The Spanish intellectual Azorín, a leading member of the 'Generation of 98', would hail Gautier for having helped the Spaniards to achieve a 'poetic understanding' of their country; less generously, the Italian critic and scholar Mario Praz would consider him largely responsible for 'faking a mannered Spain' that was later to be 'consecrated in the lyric prose style of Thos. Cook & Son Ltd'. *Journey to Spain* was a remarkable poetic synthesis of romantic attitudes towards the country, and though contributing little of originality to the Orientalist vision of the Alhambra, revealed Gautier's pictorial eye in the painterly vividness of the language, as, for instance, in his description of the sunset as viewed from the Peinador de la Reina: 'the mountains sparkle like shining mounds of rubies, topaz, and garnets; a haze of gold dust glows in the gaps, and, if workers are burning straw in the fields, as they so often do during the summer months, the wisps of smoke that rise up to the sky magically mirror the embers of the dying sun'. With brilliant scenes such as these in front of them, why, Gautier wondered, have Spanish painters tended always to darken their canvases and imitate the example of Caravaggio and other sombre artists?

Appropriately it was foreign artists and illustrators rather than Spaniards who created in the 1830s a pictorial image of the Alhambra worthy of comparison to the literary one. The first memorable artists to have worked here were John

John Frederick Lewis, whose love of the Alhambra was undoubtedly enhanced by its then picturesque inhabitants and state of romantic decay, portrayed the Palace of the Partal at a time when its arches were blocked up and its interior used as a modest domestic residence known as the Casa Sánchez.

Frederick Lewis and David Roberts, both of whom came to Spain from Britain in 1832, and were so taken in Granada by their first taste of the 'Orient' that they would later be lured over to Egypt and the Near East. Lewis was more interested in figures than in architecture, and he peopled his Alhambra scenes with Spanish types to match the picturesqueness and exoticism of the buildings. Monks and nuns reinforced British notions of Spanish fanaticism, while the colour-fully dressed *majos* and *majas* (low-class dandies) took on the roles respectively of Moorish grandees and veiled Islamic beauties. As with many travellers to Spain from this time onwards, Lewis was also fascinated by gypsies, who, conscious of their growing reputation among foreigners as the true inheritors of the Moors, had begun to exploit gullible artists and tourists with demonstrations of flamenco singing and dancing.

Similar types, but rendered diminutive by their surroundings, were also a feature of the works of Roberts, whose training as painter of architectural backdrops for the stage made him the ideal person to extend and perfect the tradition of Sublime distortions of the Alhambra. No one before him had made the towers of the

Alhambra quite so Babylonian in their proportions or given to the rooms off the Court of the Lions such a Gothic, gloomy and cavernous character. Thanks to a vision and an artistry lacking in the works of James Murphy, Roberts's popular but potentially ludicrous renditions of the Alhambra managed to be so persuasive as fantasies that the travel-writer Thomas Roscoe, whose texts they sometimes illustrated, appears to have felt no need to visit the place itself.

While Lewis and Roberts consolidated the Romantic image of the Alhambra, their French contemporary Girault de Prangey, who arrived in Granada in the same year that they did, returned to the ideals of the Academia de San Fernando in his pursuit of a more scholarly approach towards the portrayal of the monument.

David Roberts' view of the Hall of the Abencerrages displays an exaggeration of scale comparable to that of James Murphy (see page 159).

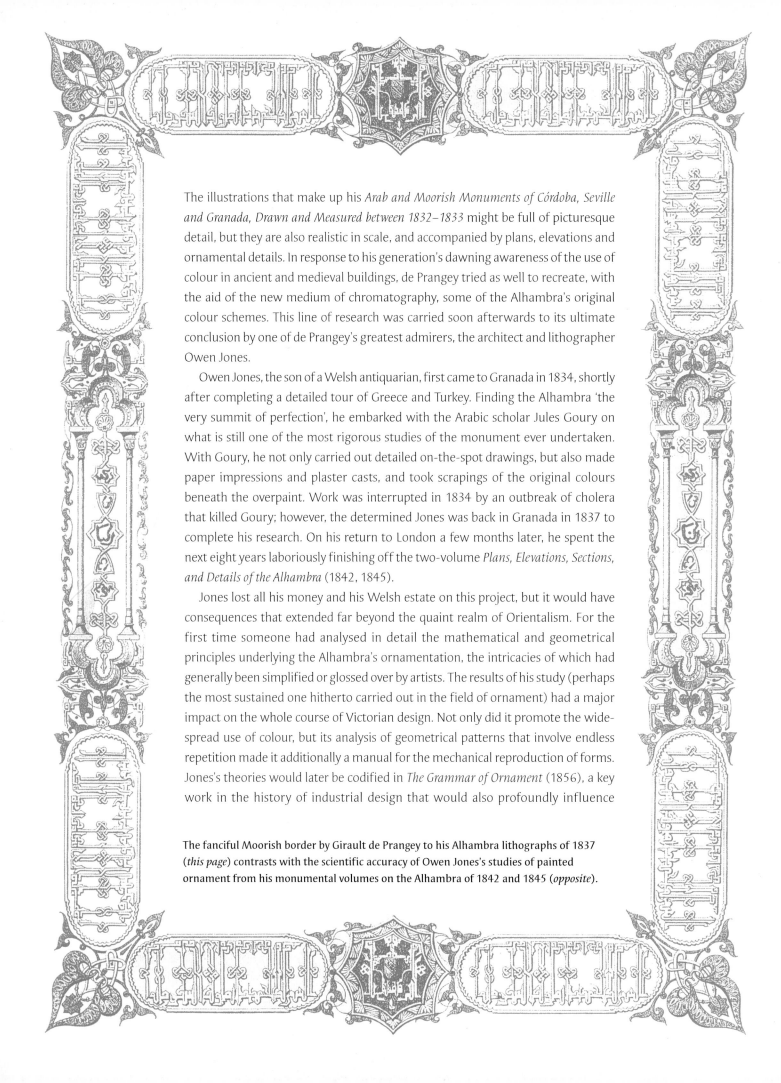

The illustrations that make up his *Arab and Moorish Monuments of Córdoba, Seville and Granada, Drawn and Measured between 1832–1833* might be full of picturesque detail, but they are also realistic in scale, and accompanied by plans, elevations and ornamental details. In response to his generation's dawning awareness of the use of colour in ancient and medieval buildings, de Prangey tried as well to recreate, with the aid of the new medium of chromatography, some of the Alhambra's original colour schemes. This line of research was carried soon afterwards to its ultimate conclusion by one of de Prangey's greatest admirers, the architect and lithographer Owen Jones.

Owen Jones, the son of a Welsh antiquarian, first came to Granada in 1834, shortly after completing a detailed tour of Greece and Turkey. Finding the Alhambra 'the very summit of perfection', he embarked with the Arabic scholar Jules Goury on what is still one of the most rigorous studies of the monument ever undertaken. With Goury, he not only carried out detailed on-the-spot drawings, but also made paper impressions and plaster casts, and took scrapings of the original colours beneath the overpaint. Work was interrupted in 1834 by an outbreak of cholera that killed Goury; however, the determined Jones was back in Granada in 1837 to complete his research. On his return to London a few months later, he spent the next eight years laboriously finishing off the two-volume *Plans, Elevations, Sections, and Details of the Alhambra* (1842, 1845).

Jones lost all his money and his Welsh estate on this project, but it would have consequences that extended far beyond the quaint realm of Orientalism. For the first time someone had analysed in detail the mathematical and geometrical principles underlying the Alhambra's ornamentation, the intricacies of which had generally been simplified or glossed over by artists. The results of his study (perhaps the most sustained one hitherto carried out in the field of ornament) had a major impact on the whole course of Victorian design. Not only did it promote the wide-spread use of colour, but its analysis of geometrical patterns that involve endless repetition made it additionally a manual for the mechanical reproduction of forms. Jones's theories would later be codified in *The Grammar of Ornament* (1856), a key work in the history of industrial design that would also profoundly influence

The fanciful Moorish border by Girault de Prangey to his Alhambra lithographs of 1837 (*this page*) contrasts with the scientific accuracy of Owen Jones's studies of painted ornament from his monumental volumes on the Alhambra of 1842 and 1845 (*opposite*).

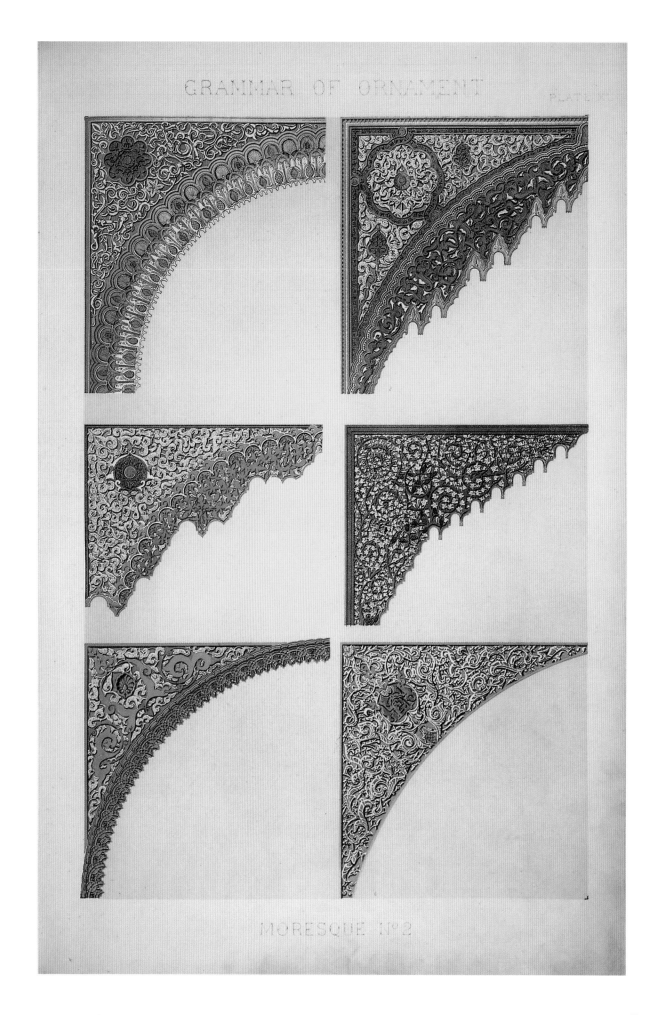

MORESQUE Nº2

20th-century abstract artists such as Piet Mondrian by showing how geometrical ornament evolved through abstracted representations of nature.

The Alhambra, thanks to Jones, became a monument that belonged as much to the industrial present as it did to the romantic past. This curious situation was not as contradictory as it might at first appear, for an immediate outcome of Jones's research was to perpetuate romantic dreams of the Alhambra through facilitating its reproduction in three dimensions. Jones himself became responsible for the first such replica when he was put in charge of the interior decoration of the main pavilion of Britain's Great Exhibition of 1851: in the middle of an ironwork hall filled with 'Alhambresque' ornament, he produced a copy of the Court of the Lions that proved so popular that it would be recreated three years later when the Crystal Palace was re-erected in the London borough of Sydenham.

This copy, adapted slightly to English tastes through the omission of the courtyard's projecting porticoes, brought the Alhambra to a much wider public than ever before, and fanned ambitions of living in settings based on the Nasrid Palaces. Under the influence of 'Alhamborough Jones', as the novelist W. M. Thackeray now called him, the commercialization and domestication of the monument gathered pace. Alhambra-inspired homes burgeoned throughout Europe and America in the late 19th century, and well into the 20th the name of the Alhambra, and elements of its architecture, would be appropriated by casinos, music halls, theatres, cinemas, Turkish baths, pieces of kitsch furniture and other places and objects intended to recreate exotic splendour and decadence for the age of mass reproduction.

It goes without saying that those who had visited the Alhambra itself could never be satisfied by even the most conscientious and convincing of pastiches. The anonymous author of a guide to the courts of the 'Sydenham Palace' admitted that the qualities that made the Alhambra so beautiful, picturesque and sublime could never be properly reproduced, as they resided in the place's atmosphere, climate, setting and hidden layers of history and legends. In Jones's Alhambra Court visitors could not hear as in Granada the 'sighs of the murdered Moors' from the Hall of the Abencerrages, nor could they find any magic in a fountain that – deprived of its original context of fragrant flowers – seemed little more than a modern pipe spouting water. The place, in fact, was so new and strident that it seemed 'like Othello dressed in a Bond Street suit'.

The only true substitute for a visit to the Alhambra was to become immersed in the romantic literary outpourings that appeared to increase rather than diminish in

In his influential *Grammar of Ornament* (*opposite*), published in 1856, Owen Jones reproduced spandrels from the Alhambra that inspired some of the 'Alhambresque' ironwork he designed in 1851 for the interior of the Crystal Palace (*above*).

intensity as the 19th century progressed. The popularity of the monument among Spaniards themselves was enormously increased with the publication in 1852 of José Zorrilla's two volumes of poems entitled *Granada*. This massive work, by the Castilian-born author of Spain's most regularly performed version of the Don Juan story, retold all the by now over-familiar legends of late 15th-century Granada with the aid of Hugo-like evocations of each of the different rooms of 'the oriental Alhambra'. To lend a greater depth to all this lyrical whimsy, Zorrilla added scholarly notes and Arabic transcriptions to his text, and even wrote a preface expressing the hope that Arabic would one day be compulsory in Spanish schools. Though this last hope was not realized, Zorrilla was at least successful in securing for the Alhambra a place of supreme importance in Spain's national consciousness. In 1889, the apotheosis of Spanish Orientalism was reached when Zorrilla was ceremoniously crowned Spain's national poet in the Alhambra. This extraordinarily well attended event was described by one of his contemporaries as being of comparable magnitude to the burial of Victor Hugo seven years earlier in Paris.

Zorrilla's fame was largely limited to Spain, unlike that of his younger Italian contemporary Edmondo de Amicis, whose book *Spain and the Spaniards* (1879) was the most successful travelogue on Spain since Gautier's. It was also the most tiresomely effusive. In his descriptions of the Alhambra he piled on adjectives, metaphors and exclamation marks with a profusion that climaxed with a half-page sentence to convey the first impact on him of the Court of the Lions, which for him was '. . . a forest of columns . . . a prodigious richness . . . a great pavilion of lace . . . a capricious order of little things . . . an amorous grace, an extravagance, a delirium, the fancy of an imaginative child, the dream of an angel, a madness, a nameless something . . .'

But behind this dense coating of phrases was an absence of original observations on the Alhambra, which de Amicis described, like hundreds of other writers before him, as an expression not of 'power, glory and grandeur' but rather of 'love and voluptuousness'. More irritating still was the way he pretended to have felt duped by his guide on being taken up to the Alhambra through the Gate of Justice and finding nothing at first but a 'disgraceful' modern palace and a group of 'wretched houses'. 'Well, then, this great name of Alhambra is only one of the usual charlatan-like hyperboles of poets,' he concluded before being taken into the Court of the Myrtles and finding that the 'Alhambra had already begun to exercize upon me that deep and mysterious fascination from which none escape'. Overcome now by a feeling that he had been here before, he attributed this sensation to having unknowingly imagined the monument when he had fallen in love at the age of sixteen, 'when desires are dreams and visions'.

No one reading de Amicis's account of a deserted Alhambra familiar only from dreams could possibly have guessed that the place he was describing – easily accessible now by train – had already become one of the most reproduced, written about and visited monuments in Europe. A Tunisian traveller of the 1880s, al-Wardani, was struck by the number of painters at work within its courtyards and by the 'convoys of tourists, mainly English, who visit this enchanting place'.

'It is the dead of night: silent and deserted, The Alhambra, jewel of the east, Is hidden in the shadows; Granada lies at her feet, silent too, And dark and sad and lonely.'

From José Zorrilla's *Granada, an Oriental Poem*.

The long-bearded poet José Zorrilla (fifth from the right) stands among admirers in the middle of the Court of the Lions. The occasion was his crowning in 1889 as Spain's national poet.

Photographers, catering to the new fashion of having one's photo taken in Moorish costume, waited dressed as Moors within the Court of the Lions, holding robes and turbans for visitors to put on. By the late 1880s the carnival atmosphere within the Nasrid Palaces had become such that photographers were no longer permitted inside; instead they set up studios with mock-ups of the Court of the Lions in Granada itself, and in front of the Palace of Charles V.

Elsewhere on the Alhambra hill hotels were built to console those frustrated travellers nostalgic for the days when Irving and Ford had been able to imagine themselves sleeping in the company of sultans. A modest inn named after Irving was transformed in the 1860s into a hotel considered by some the most luxurious in Spain. Among its guests during this decade were the Swiss Rothschilds, whose patronage of the hotel's guide and former bell boy made possible the opening of the nearby Pensión Alhambra, on a site alongside the present *parador*. In 1912, a later owner of this pension became the first director of the Hotel Alhambra Palace, a giant neo-Moorish construction that totally destroyed the idyllic views to the south once famously enjoyed from the home of the British consul.

As tourism escalated, Granada came increasingly to lose its original Moorish aspect. The burning down of the Alcaicería bazaar in 1843 coincided with the wilful demolition in the Albaicín of the Maristan, the finest survival anywhere of a medieval Islamic hospital. Granada, a place described by Ford as stagnating in 'bookless ignorance', destroyed even more of its Moorish past in the late 19th century, when renewed commercial prosperity (resulting in part from the tourist boom) led to the flattening of medieval houses to make way for the Gran Vía de Colón, a boulevard lined with pompous office and apartment blocks.

In the meantime the Alhambra itself was changing no less significantly, as more and more of the decayed original fabric was having to be replaced by modern restoration. A Frenchman had complained in 1792 that English

The art historian Albert F. Calvert, a prolific writer on Spain's Moorish antiquities, follows the example of many of Granada's visitors and inhabitants by posing as a Moor in one of the town's several photographic studios set up for this purpose.

visitors were removing stones from the Alhambra without being stopped by the Spaniards; in 1874, four years after the place had been declared Spain's first National Monument, the Baron Charles Davillier, visiting the Nasrid Palaces in the company of the artist Gustave Doré, was shocked by coming across a foreign 'Vandal' happily removing a ceramic tile 'as if he was doing the most natural thing in the world'.

This incident (recorded by Doré in an illustration) was perhaps all the more surprising given that a serious modern restoration campaign was by then already under way. Later additions and alterations considered now to be inauthentic were being replaced by modern structures, while new tiles and stuccowork were filling up the gaps left by centuries of neglect. The fears of earlier travellers that the Alhambra would not survive the 19th century had been allayed, but at a cost – the Alhambra was in danger of becoming as much of a replica as the ones still proliferating in the wake of Owen Jones.

The novelist Alexandre Dumas had prayed in 1847 that the Alhambra would either remain standing or, in the case of falling down completely, be left as a ruin: 'I prefer,' he wrote, 'a corpse to a mummy.' In 1890 this last wish would almost be granted following the most dramatic event in the Alhambra's later history.

At ten o'clock on the night of 15 September, a fire broke out under the north gallery of the Court of the Myrtles. The flames, first seen by a night watchman in the Albaicín, rose high into the sky, and soon threatened to engulf the whole complex. The shout of 'Fire in the Alhambra!' spread around Granada, and the bells of the watch tower were rung loudly, as they would have been in the past to alert the townspeople to the advance of an enemy. Many, such as the local historian and patriot Francisco de Paula Valladar, rushed up to the monument to see what could be done to put out the flames. Only after seven hours was the fire finally quelled, to reveal a sight that, in the words of Valladar, made 'tears stream from your eyes and blood boil in your heart'.

Typically for the Alhambra, even this well-recorded event soon became shrouded in myth. The fire was almost certainly the work of an arsonist, but the culprit was never found. Much speculation ensued as to who could have committed such an appalling crime, and Valladar was convinced that had the arsonist been found red-handed, he or she would almost certainly have been lynched. Blame was inevitably placed by the Granadans on one of the Alhambra's 'envious' foreign visitors. In the end the most popular belief was that the fire was an act of revenge carried out by a mysterious group of Moors who preferred to see their beloved Alhambra destroyed than have it remain in the hands of the infidel.

The extent of reconstruction made necessary by the fire did nothing to stop the Alhambra's ever growing popularity, or indeed lessen its inspiration to artists, writers and, increasingly, musicians. The Russian composer Mikhail Glinka, who came to Granada in 1847 and befriended a gypsy musician, initiated a whole tradition of musicians taking their inspiration from gypsy and other Spanish themes. Out of this was born so-called 'Alhambrista' music, which was often written without any direct experience of Granada, as was the case not only with Debussy's *Soirées en Granade* and *La Puerta del Vino*, but also, and more curiously, with Manuel de Falla's *In the Generalife*, one of the nocturnes from his celebrated piece for piano and orchestra, *In the Gardens of Spain*.

Gustave Doré's witty portrayal of a tourist removing part of the Alhambra's decoration is unfortunately based on a real incident observed by the artist and his companion Charles Davillier on a tour of the monument in 1874.

Falla fell in love with Granada long before going there. His affair with the town began in Paris, where he made friends with Debussy and met in 1907 a Granadan guitarist called Ángel Barrios, whom he came to know while attending musical soirées in the Parisian home of the Catalan composer Isaac Albéniz. Barrios, whose dark skin and big moustache made him seem Moorish to his foreign critics, was a passionate advocate of his home town, which he said he would not exchange for any other place in the world, not even London or Paris. In Albéniz's apartment he performed music that was consciously intended to reawaken memories of the Alhambra in the then seriously ill Albéniz, who knew that he would never be able to return there. A whole new imaginary world opened up for Falla, as he sat entranced listening to Barrios's guitar, and to the nostalgic musings that all references to the Alhambra have tended so often to induce.

Not until 1915 did Falla finally get to know the Alhambra, which he saw for the first time one April morning while touring southern Spain with a theatre company. One of his travelling companions, the writer María Lejárraga, recalled in her memoirs how she had insisted that the composer keep his eyes closed until she had led him into the Hall of the Ambassadors. After finally being allowed to open them again, the composer shouted out 'Ah! Ah!' in a way that his companion would never forget: 'It was almost a shriek,' she wrote, unsure as to whether this had been one of pure delight, or one of surprise on discovering how closely the place matched his musical imaginings of it. '"Thank you!", was all that he said, returning once again to his thoughts.'

Following the death of his parents in Madrid in 1919 Falla came back again to Granada, this time with the intention of settling here for good. Before moving eventually into a charming small villa near the Hotel Alhambra Palace, he stayed in the Pensión Alhambra, which was a few minutes walk away from the Polinario, an inn and shop owned by Barrios's father Antonio. Crowded today mainly with tour groups, this establishment, directly in front of the Alhambra's former mosque, was in Falla's time a centre of local literary and artistic life, and a meeting place for all the many distinguished cultural visitors to the town.

A small museum, recently installed within the ruins of the mosque's baths, contains mementos of the Polinario. Among these is a portrait of Antonio Barrios by his painter friend John Singer Sargent and a framed document nominating Barrios as the 'Artistic Consul to the Alhambra'. This document's distinguished signatories include not only Sargent (who signed himself here as '*Un Granadino de América*'), but also many of the leading Spanish artists of the early 20th century, such as the Córdoban painter of sultry Andalucían beauties Julio Romero de Torres, Picasso's first teacher López Mezquita, and the prominent Barcelona painters Ramón Casas and Santiago Rusiñol. However, together with Falla, the Spanish associate of the Polinario circle who is best remembered today outside Spain is the native Granadan poet, Federico García Lorca.

OPPOSITE The Granadan-born painter López Mezquita, one of the finest Spanish artists closely associated with the Alhambra, portrayed the Court of the Myrtles when its northern gallery was still being restored following the fire damage of 1890 in this painting entitled *Patio de los Arrayanes* (1904).

ABOVE The composer Manuel de Falla is seen here at his desk in his small house on the Alhambra hill.

Lorca's love of the Alhambra was central to his life and to his work; but his writings on the monument, despite the originality and modernity in their resonant turn of phrase, exemplify the persistence in the 20th century of romantic attitudes dating back to the days of Irving and Gautier. The latter's *Journey to Spain* was indeed greatly enjoyed by the young Lorca, as was the poetry of Zorrilla, whose spirit he described in one of his early prose pieces on Granada as floating 'above the copper and bronze towers of the Alhambra'.

As with his romantic predecessors, Lorca could not think of Islamic Granada in terms other than as a paradise, of which the Alhambra was its glowing heart. The Alhambra was for him the 'aesthetic axis' of Granada, and a place whose arabesque intricacies and intimacies were expressive of a poetic Granadan soul on which the Christians had tried to impose such alien monstrosities as the Palace of Charles V.

Romantic adulation of the Moorish past was combined in Lorca with an elitism as great as that of romantic travellers: whereas they claimed that no one could understand the Alhambra who had not stayed there, he felt that the monument's soul would be for ever closed to 'Tío turista', and could never be fully open to those who had not been brought up under its shadow. Fortunately he also had a sense of humour, which allowed him to make fun of his Moorish pretensions by inventing a ridiculous, myrtle-eating Granadan called Don Alhambro.

Lorca was able to talk about 'the comic oriental opera of Granada', while being at

The poet García Lorca poses with friends next to the pool of the Palace of the Partal (*below*). His child-like rapture with the Alhambra is evident in his drawing *Vista general de la Alhambra* (*opposite*), which he used to try and persuade a friend to come and stay in Granada.

the same time an enthusiastic participant in the whole charade. He loved dressing up in Moorish costume, and, like many tourists and fellow Granadans, he and his friends often had themselves photographed in such attire, notably in 1918, when, under his inspiration, they all enacted in the Polinario a Moorish tale involving secret treasure. Fascination with the Moorish past took on a more serious form four years later, when Lorca and Falla decided to organize within the Alhambra a festival of gypsy *cante jondo*: in so doing they perpetuated the romantic delusion that, in the absence of real Moors, the best alternatives were the gypsies.

Lorca's uncritical acceptance of the Romantic image of Islamic Granada was his way of escaping from the ugly reality of the modern town, which he was constantly attacking. In one of his last interviews, given just before the eve of the Spanish Civil War, he famously spoke about 1492 as a 'disastrous event. An admirable civilization, and a poetry, architecture and delicacy unique in the world – all were lost, to give way to an impoverished, cowed town, a wasteland populated by the worst bourgeoisie in Spain today.' Comments such as these did not endear him to the more reactionary families in Granada, and ensured that he met a death as violent as that of the Moorish poets of the Alhambra whom he so admired. By strange coincidence, he was

Vista general de la Alhambra
Federico García Lorca.
1928

gallo

herido   Llanca   (don Jorge) ......   Ahora es la hora de visitar

la **bella** ciudad de Granada.

Todo el día ha llovido y ha chapoteado la lluvia en raíces y cristales. El Otoño ha llegado. Ya la población está animadísima. La Universidad abre sus puertas.

La Alhambra y los jardines están en su justo punto poético. Dentro de cuatro días comenzarán a dorarse las hojas.

¿Tú en serio pensabas venir? ¿O fué puro juego y deseo de este viaje? Hasta ahora yo no te había dicho que vinieras porque el verano es la peor hora de esta ciudad.

Si pensabas venir, puedes contemplar ya esta maravilla. Obras que el invierno es mi mejor vestido.

Granada es la ciudad más económica de Andalucía. Se puede vivir en ella relativamente por poco dinero. ¿Qué te parece?

Contesta. Contéstame.

— río Dauro.

Adiós. Un abrazo muy cariñoso de tu mejor

Federico

assassinated in a celebrated Moorish location famed for its natural beauty and haunted by memories of Ibn al-Khatib, who had had a villa there and wrote verse in praise of a local spring known as the Fountain of Tears.

The idyllic vision of the Alhambra that Lorca had so actively supported was already being challenged during his lifetime. Lytton Strachey, who visited the monument in 1919, was so utterly dismayed that he recommended Virginia and Leonard Woolf never to go there: 'It's Death! Death!' he moaned. This opinion seems partly to have been shared by his perverse Hispanist friend Gerald Brenan, who had first seen the Alhambra under a steady drizzle, when it had appeared to him 'shoddy and bedraggled, like a gypsy girl sitting under a damp hedge'. Later he described the monument as 'a glorified gazebo'.

The most sustained and seriously argued attack on the Alhambra appeared in 1928 in Mario Praz's wonderfully acerbic book *Unromantic Spain* (the original Italian title was even better: *Penisola Pentagonale*). Praz, an Italian critic and academic with a reputation for diabolic powers, believed that the Alhambra could never be Romantic in the true sense of the word, for he found it lacked the necessary element of variety and surprise: the ultimate effect of all its profuse ornamentation was for him one of profound monotony.

The prejudices of a classical education were clearly as strong in Praz as his delight in shocking people. But his book makes a refreshing read after all the romantic gush on the Alhambra that he so brilliantly satirized: 'Reader,' he wrote, 'I did not take up my abode between the magic walls of the Alhambra for four days and as many nights, with the tacit consent of the authorities, neither did I dwell there for several months attended by houris and escorted by valets descended from the Moorish kings ... While visiting the Alhambra I did not tremble like an aspen leaf ... while leaving it I did not bid farewell to all the illusions of youth and to that love which will never live again.'

The attacks on the Alhambra by Strachey, Brenan and Praz turned out to be isolated phenomena rather than the early symptoms of a turn in the monument's critical fortunes. The Alhambra continued merely to grow in popularity, and to prove itself capable of being reinterpreted by different cultural generations. The graphic artist M. C. Escher spent a long period there in 1936 fascinated by the metamorphic possibilities of ornament: his study of the way in which each ornament merged into another one, and each line

The popular British artist Sir Muirhead Bone portrayed the Court of the Lions when it was undergoing yet another major restoration campaign. This illustration appeared in his wife Gertrude's book *Days in Old Spain* (1938).

delineated both an inner and an outer space, was fundamental to the evolution of his art and to his theories of the representation of infinity. It also provided a rational explanation of the enchanted nature of the Alhambra.

Le Corbusier, meanwhile, was interested in the architecture's flexible and fluid arrangement of space, and in the breakdown between interior and exterior. These aspects of the monument were also taken up by the group of Spanish architects who got together in 1954 to publish *El manifiesto de la Alhambra*. Thanks to this work the monument that had inspired so many eclectic pastiches became, curiously, a model to young architects who wished to break away from the historicism of the early years of General Franco's rule and encourage the spread of modernism in Spain.

Other, more banal factors have contributed in recent years to the spectacular escalation in the number of tourists visiting the Alhambra – the development of the Costa del Sol from the 1950s onwards, the dramatic improvement in road links between the coast and Granada, and even the publicity generated by President Clinton's visit in 1996. It is doubtful whether the vast majority of these visitors take much of an intellectual interest in the monument, the appeal of which has remained essentially an emotional one. Sentimental attitudes towards the Moorish past remain as prevalent as ever, even if they have become confused since the 1980s with political correctness.

In 1936, when Spain was on the verge of civil war, the graphic artist M. C. Escher visited Granada and became absorbed in a study of the Alhambra's intricate ornamentation. His famous illusionistic puzzle *Reptiles* (1943) reflects his fascination with the way in which each ornamental line delineates both an inner and an outer space.

Perhaps the most striking phenomena in recent Spanish history have been the romantic emphasis on the country's Islamic heritage and the fashion for all things Moorish. Granadan intellectuals gather each year on 2 January to protest at the annual ringing of bells to celebrate the taking of the Alhambra in 1492; in 1992 a muezzin managed to slip in by night into the complex and call the faithful to prayer from the heights of the Alcazaba's watchtower.

Growing numbers of North African Muslims and European converts to Islam have been moving into the Albaicín, where they and western sympathizers have opened Moorish tea rooms, bakeries, bookshops and even a garish imitation of the Alhambra's baths. Throughout Spain, and much of Mediterranean Europe, Moorish names are still being given to new bars and restaurants, and pastiches of the Alhambra continue to appear, often in the most unexpected places. Marbella's most fashionable discothèque – situated in between the town's mosque and the palace of the Arabian king – has walls suggestive of those of the Alcazaba, as well as a dance floor inspired by the Court of the Lions. A faithful, life-size replica of the entire Alhambra is currently being built in Saudi Arabia.

Romantic travellers who worried about the Alhambra's future might not be entirely happy with what has happened to the monument today. For the selfish few an Alhambra falling into ruins seems preferable to a shiningly restored and over-crowded place to which access is ever more restricted. Yet, paradoxically for a Spain so conscious now of its Islamic past, the poignant conditions of neglect that touched the hearts of romantic visitors to Moorish monuments are still apparent in some of the Alhambra's hidden corners, as they are in many of the other surviving relics of Nasrid Spain.

Shock, nostalgia and a sense of discovery can be felt even today in places such as the Moorish castle at Las Gabias, where rubbish, graffiti and the skeletons of birds litter rooms decorated with exquisite stuccowork from the days of Muhammad V. But in terms of sheer unexpectedness, nothing quite matches the sight of the projected national museum of Moorish art, which was built above the Generalife in the 1980s and then abandoned for political reasons. Ceilings and original plasterwork from the Alhambra have been left to gather dust in a setting that has already become, disgracefully, a modern ruin.

Ultimately, the Alhambra remains an enigma. Though few other monuments have attracted so much attention over the last two centuries, the unanswered questions continue to accumulate. The reality of the Alhambra will perhaps never be fully within our grasp; but the mythology that has grown up around it still exerts a powerful grip on our imaginations. It was as a universal myth rather than as a mortal monument that the Alhambra was glorified in the closing pages of Salman Rushdie's recent novel, *The Moor's Last Sigh*, which gave new life to the tired legends of Boabdil and the nostalgic longings that the collapse of Moorish Spain always inspires:

'And so I sit here in the last light, upon this stone, among these olive trees, gazing out across a valley towards a distant hill; and there it stands, the glory of the Moors, their triumphant masterpiece and their last redoubt. The Alhambra, Europe's red fort, sister to Delhi's and Agra's – the palace of interlocking forms and secret wisdom, of pleasure-courts and water-gardens, that monument to a lost possibility that nevertheless has gone on standing, long after its conquerors have fallen; like a testament to lost but sweetest love, to the love that endures beyond defeat, beyond annihilation, beyond despair; to the defeated love that is greater than what defeats it, to that most profound of our needs, to our need for flowing together, for putting an end to frontiers, for the dropping of the boundary of the self.'

Joaquín Sorolla, a Valencian-born artist of vividly coloured outdoor scenes, was so obsessed with the Alhambra that he partly recreated its spirit in his house and garden in Madrid. This view of the Alhambra from the Albaicín, *Granada, November 1909*, was one of a large number of oil sketches of Granada he made in that year.

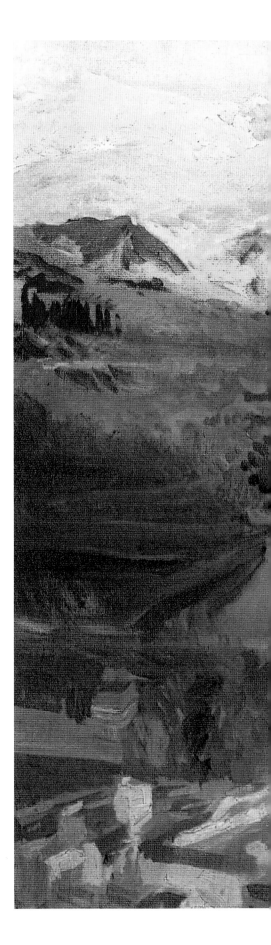

PLAN OF THE ALHAMBRA

CHRONOLOGY OF ISLAMIC SPAIN

409 Collapse of Roman power in Spain.

414 The Visigoths cross into Spain from the Pyrenees.

c. 554 Toledo is chosen as the Spanish capital.

456 Visigothic rule is extended throughout Spain.

636 Death of the prophet Muhammad.

636–c. 700 Rapid expansion of Islam following Muhammad's death. Muslim armies conquer the Berbers of north-west Africa by the end of the seventh century.

711 The Arab general Tariq Ibn Ziryab lands at Gibraltar with an army of Berber troops.

718 Christian victory at Covadonga, in northern Spain, initiates the Reconquest, c. 800–c. 1100. As the Christian Reconquest spreads southwards, Christian Spain eventually divides into the kingdoms of Asturias, Léon, Barcelona, Aragón and Castile.

720 Islamic reconstruction of the Roman walls and bridge at Córdoba. Foundation of Spain's first Islamic cemetery.

756 Arrival in Spain from Morocco of Prince Abd al-Rahman, the sole surviving member of the Umayyad dynasty of Damascus.

784 Work begins on the Great Mosque or Mezquita at Córdoba.

929 Abd al-Rahman III proclaims himself caliph, or 'leader of the faithful'. Córdoba becomes the caliphate of the West.

936 Foundation of Medina Azahara.

961–6 Extension of the Great Mosque at Córdoba by al-Hakam II.

1009 Sacking of Medina Azahara by the Berbers.

1030 Collapse of the Umayyad dynasty. Islamic Spain is broken up into independent kingdoms known as *taifas*, the most powerful of which is Seville. Granada, of relatively minor importance at this time, is ruled by the Berber Zirids.

1085 The Christian king Alfonso VI of Léon captures Toledo.

1086 Arrival in Spain of the Almoravids, a fanatical Berber sect.

1091 The Almoravids capture Seville.

1095 Death of the Sevillian king al-Mutamid in the Moroccan town of Agmat.

1145 End of the Almoravid domination in Spain.

1147 A new Berber dynasty, the Almohads, conquer Seville.

1212 The combined Christian forces of Castile, Léon, Aragon and Navarre defeat the Almohads at the Battle of Las Navas de Tolosa.

1217 Uprising led by Ibn Hud in south-eastern Spain.

1231 Al-Ahmar Ibn Nasr, the founder of the Nasrid dynasty, becomes governor of his native town of Arjona, to the north of Granada.

1237 Ibn Nasr siezes Granada, which becomes, eight years later, the capital of his kingdom.

1238 Death of Ibn Hud by poison.

1248 After taking Córdoba and Murcia, Ferdinand III of Castile and Léon captures Seville. Muslim rule in Spain is reduced to the sultanate of Granada, which stretches west to Gibraltar and east to Almería.

1252 Death of Ferdinand III; succession of Alfonso X.

1273 Death of Ibn Nasr.

1302–9 Reign of Muhammad III; construction of the Palace of the Partal.

1313 Birth in Loja of the poet, polymath and politician Ibn al-Khatib.

1314–25 Reign of Ismail I; creation of the original Mexuar.

1314 Work begins on the Generalife.

1325–33 Reign of Muhammad IV.

1333–54 Reign of Yusuf I; creation of most of the Palace of Comares.

1333 Birth of the poet and politician Ibn Zamrak to an iron-worker from the Albaicín.

1340 Defeat of the Islamic forces at the Battle of Río Salado.

1354–91 Reign of Muhammad V; completion of the Palace of Comares and the creation of the Palace of the Lions and Sala de la Barca.

1354 Yusuf I is stabbed to death by a deranged slave while praying in the Great Mosque in Granada.

1359 Muhammad V, unseated by a coup while staying in the Generalife, takes refuge in Morocco, where he is joined by his vizier Ibn al-Khatib.

1359–60 Reign of Ismail II.

1360-2 Reign of Muhammad VI.

1362 Reinstatement of Muhammad V in Granada.

1369 Muhammad V recaptures Algeciras from the Christians, a victory commemorated in various inscriptions in the Alhambra.

1371 Flight of Ibn al-Khatib to Morocco; Ibn Zamrak is elected vizier in his place.

1374 Assassination of Ibn al-Khatib in Fez.

1391 Death of Muhammad V.

1392 Assassination of Ibn Zamrak in Granada.

1392–1408 Reign of Muhammad VII; creation of the Tower of the Infantas.

1464–82 Reign of Abul-Hasan.

1469 Christian Spain is unified following the marriage of Isabella I of Castile to Ferdinand II of Aragón (the two monarchs are commonly known thereafter as the Catholic monarchs).

1478 Severe flooding in Granada during the middle of a massive military parade organized by Abul-Hasan.

1482 Christian capture of Alhama in Granada provokes the last stage of the Reconquest.

1482–92 Reign of Muhammad XII (known as Boabdil or El Rey Chico), Granada's last sultan.

1492 Boabdil surrenders the Alhambra to the Catholic monarchs Ferdinand and Isabella.

1499 Arrival in Granada of the fanatical Cardinal Cisneros as Archbishop; beginnings of the forceful conversion of Granada's Islamic population to Christianity.

1499–1501 First Morisco uprising.

1522 A serious earthquake creates extensive damage in the Nasrid Palaces.

1526 Arrival in Granada of the Holy Roman Emperor, Charles V; work begins on the Palace of Charles V.

1568–71 Second Morisco uprising. The Moriscos are banned from the former kingdom of Granada.

1590 Explosion of a powder factory in the Albaicín sparks off a fire in the Alhambra.

1609 Expulsion of the Moriscos from Spain.

FURTHER READING

Although the literature on Islamic Spain is vast and rapidly expanding, a high proportion of it comprises a mixture of specialist studies of essentially scholarly interest or popular works of strong sentimental character. One of the rare historical introductions to this period that manages to be authoritative, accessible and thought-provoking is Richard Fletcher's *Moorish Spain* (London, 1992), which should be read in conjunction with Titus Burckhardt's stimulating and thematically arranged survey of Hispano-Moorish culture, *Moorish Culture in Spain* (New York and Toronto, 1972).

Both the history and the culture of al-Andalus are concisely if rather drearily summarized in W. Montgomery Watt's *A History of Islamic Spain* (Edinburgh, 1965). Much more detailed is Anwar Chejne's inexplicably neglected *Muslim Spain. Its History and Culture* (Minneapolis, 1974), which is especially good on literature and philosophy. Essays on most aspects of Islamic Spain are featured in the two large volumes edited by Salma Khadra Jayyusi, *The Legacy of Muslim Spain* (Leiden, 1994); among the various studies featured here is James Dickie's exemplary 'Granada: A Case Study of Arab Urbanism in Muslim Spain'.

The two classic surveys of Islamic Granada are Miguel Ángel Ladero Quesada's *Granada. Historia de un país Islámico 1232–1571* (Madrid, 1989) and Rachel Arié's *L'Espagne musulmane au temps des Nasrides 1232–1492* (Paris, 1990), both of which are exciting and readable works of scholarship. L. P. Harvey's *Islamic Spain 1250–1500* (Chicago and London, 1990) is similarly impressive, but concentrates largely on this period's political and military history.

A wonderfully lively contemporary account of Zirid Granada is Amin T. Tibi's edition of *The Tibyan. Memoirs of 'Abd Allah ibn Buluggin, last Zirid amir of Granada* (Leiden, 1986). Early traveller's accounts of Granada are brought together in Francisco Javier Simonet's *Descripción del Reino de Granada* (Granada, 1872), García Mercedal's three-volumed *Viajes de extranjeros por España y Portugal desde los tiempos más remotos hasta fines del siglo XV* (Madrid, 1952) and Cristina Viñes's *Granada en los libros de viaje* (Granada, 1982). The best modern edition of Ibn al-Khatib's *The Shining Rays of the Full Moon* (*Al-Lamha al-badriyya*) is Emilio Molina and José María Casciaro's *Historia de los Reyes de la Alhambra* (Granada, 1998), which also includes an excellent detailed introduction to the poet's life. Ibn al-Khatib's devious rival Ibn Zamrak is the subject of García Gómez's *Ibn Zamrak. El poeta de la Alhambra* (Madrid, 1943).

The Alhambra's leading restorer this century, Leopoldo Torres Balbas, was also the author of two pioneering studies on the art and architecture of Islamic Spain, 'Arte almohade, arte nazarí, arte mudéjar' in *Ars Hispaniae, IV* (Madrid, 1949) and *Ciudades hispano-musulmanas* (2 vols., Madrid, 1971). The weighty exhibition catalogue *Al-Andalus, The Arts of Islamic Spain* (The Metropolitan Museum of Art, New York and the Alhambra, Granada, 1992) contains much of the more recent research on the subject, as does the later catalogue, *Arte islámico en Granada. Propuesta para un Museo de la Alhambra* (Palace of Charles V, Granada, 1995). A good, well-illustrated history in English of Hispano-Moorish architecture is Marianne Barruand and Achim Bednorz's *Moorish Architecture in Andalusia* (Cologne, 1992). Godfrey Goodwin's *Islamic Spain* (London, 1990) is a useful architectural guide.

Owen Jones and J. Goury's *Elevations. Sections and Details of the Alhambra* (London, 1842–5) remains unequalled as an illustrated record of the Alhambra's decorations, while Antonio Gallego y Burín's celebrated *Granada: guía artística e histórica de la ciudad* (Madrid, 1961) contains what is still the most detailed guidebook coverage of the monument. But for a brilliant analysis of the Alhambra's deeper significance, and for a massively researched scholarly account of its decoration and architecture, the reader should turn respectively to Oleg Grabar's highly controversial *The Alhambra* (London, 1978) and to Antonio Fernández-Puertas's beautifully produced, but at times almost impenetrable, book of the same title (London, 1997; a second volume, on the function and meaning of the different rooms, is currently in preparation). Other important studies of the Alhambra include Frederick P. Bargebuhr's fascinating, if not wholly convincing, *The Alhambra: A Cycle of Studies on the Eleventh Century in Moorish Spain* (Berlin, 1968), Antonio Fernández-Puertas's characteristically thorough *La fachada del Palacio Comares: situación, función y génesis* (Granada, 1980) and Earl Rosenthal's *The Palace of Charles V in Granada* (Princeton, New Jersey, 1985).

The history of the Alhambra under its Christian governors is given in Cristina Viñes Millet's *La Alhambra de Granada. Tres siglos de historia* (Granada, 1982), while the impact of the monument on the romantic imagination is vividly discussed in Tania Raquejo's *El palacio encantado. La Alhambra y el arte Británico* (Madrid, 1990). Two curiosities are Francisco de Paula Valladar's disturbing but little-known account of the disastrous 1890 fire, *El Incendio de la Alhambra* (Granada, 1890), and the famous *Manifiesto de la Alhambra* of 1953 (re-issued in Granada in 1990, with an introduction by Fernando Chueca Goitia) – a testimony to the influence of the monument on the architectural avant-garde of the post-war years.

INDEX

G

gardens 38, 44, *44*, 128, 146, *146*, 149, *149*
Gate of the Esplanade/Gate of Justice *see* Bab al-Shari'a
Gate of the Seven Floors *see* Bab al-Ghadur
Gautier, Théophile 6, 66, 67, 90, 98, 146, 165, 166
Generalife 28, *44*, *61*, 146, *146*, 149, *149*, *152*, 158
geometrical ornament 168, 171
Germana de Foix 87
Gibraltar 10, 29, 47
Gilpin, William 158
Glinka, Mikhail 175
Gothic architecture 87, *87*, *142*, 158
Goury, Jules 168
Grabar, Oleg 29, 67
Grammar of Ornament (Owen Jones) 168, *168*, *171*
Granada 15, 18, 22, 25
   city layout 35
   destruction of Moorish past 174
   Golden Age 28, 29, 31, 34, 44
   Granadan characteristics 34
   Islamic Granada 18, 28, 35
   Nasrid Granada 28, 29, 47, 156
   population 34
   Reconquest of Granada 50, 51, 156
   suburbs 38
Granada Cathedral 65
Granada (José Zorrilla) 172, *172*
Great Mosque (Córdoba) 12, *12*, 15, 53
Great Mosque (Granada) 35
Guadix 48
gypsies 58, 167, 175, 178

H

Hall of the Abencerrages *74*, 120, *120*, 159, *167*
Hall of the Ambassadors *4*, 58, 77, 98, 101, *101*, *104*, 106
Hall of the Kings 58, 124, *124*, *127*
Hall of the Two Sisters 120, 128, *128*, *130*
hammam 38, *40*, 68, 106, *106*, 108, *108*
Handbook to Spain (Richard Ford) 7, 164
Hare, Augustus 7
harem *118*, 120
Herrera, Juan de 53

Hotel Alhambra Palace 174
Hugo, Victor 162–3, 172

I

Ibn al-Khatib 10, 25, 31, *31*, 32, 33, 34–5, 38, 44, 68, 106, *108*, *118*, 128, 140, 146, 180
Ibn al-Yayyab 76, 140, *142*
Ibn Battuta 44
Ibn Gabirol 19, 112
Ibn Hud al-Judhami 23, 25
Ibn Luyun 149, *152*
Ibn Muza al-Razi, Ahmad Ibn Muhammad 15
Ibn Nasr *see* Muhammad I
Ibn Zamrak 31–2, *32*, 33, *33*, 34, 44, 70, 76, 87, *97*, 112, *114*, 128, *128*, *130*, 146
inscriptions 28
Irving, Washington 15, 65, 67, 98, 112, 124, 128, *134*, 141, 160, 163, *163*
Isabel of Portugal 53, *61*, 136
Isabel de Solís 47, *142*
Islamic Spain 10, 12
Ismail I 28, 80, 90, 106
Ismail II 70, *127*

J

Jacob, William 159
Jaén 25
Jews 10, 18, 19, 34
Joan the Mad 51
Jones, Owen 168, *168*, 171, *171*
Journey to Spain (Théophile Gautier) 165, 166, 178

K

Koran 77, *82*, 87, 101
Kufic script 76, 128

L

La Higueruela, Battle of *47*
Las Gabias 182
Las Navas de Tolosa 23
Last of the Abencerrages (Chateaubriand) 160, 162, *162*, 163

Le Corbusier 181
Lejárraga, María 177
Les Orientales (Victor Hugo) 162–3
Lewis, John Frederick *58*, 87, *136*, 166–7, *166*
Loja 31, 48
Lorca, Federico García *53*, 67, 177–8, *178*, 180

M

Machuca, Pedro 53, *53*, 56, 70, *72*
Madinat al-Hamra 26
madrasas 32, 35
Maristan hospital 38, *139*, 174
Marwan II 12
Medina Azahara 15, *15*, 18, 28
Mendoza, Hurtado de 66
Merinids 26, 29, 47
Mexuar *9*, 70, *72*, 77, 80, *80*, *82*, 87, 128
Mezquita, López 177, *177*
mihrab 98
Mirador de Lindaraxa 128, *130*
miradors 74, 149, *149*
Moclín *15*, 48
Monastery of San Francisco 136
Mondrian, Piet 171
Mondújar, Duke of 58
Montalvo, Garci Rodríguez de 156
Moorish sensuality 108, 156
Moriscos 51, *51*, 57, 58, 156
mosque architecture 12
mosques 12, 15, 35, 53, 136, 149
Mozart, Wolfgang Amadeus 157
Muhammad al-Zaghal 48
Muhammad I (Ibn Nasr) 23, 25, *25*, 26, 68
Muhammad II 26, 31
Muhammad III 28, 136
Muhammad V 28, 29, 31, 33, 38, 67, 70, 77, 80, 87, 90, 106, 110, 136, *136*
Muhammad VI 70, *127*
Muhammad IX 120
Müntz, Johann Heinrich *157*
Münzer, Hieronymus 58, 146, 156
muqarnas 76, 87, 98, 101, 120, *120*, 124
Murdoch, Nina 110
Murphy, James Cavanagh 158, 159
muslimah 12
muwalladun 12